Writing for
Quick Cash

Books by Loriann Hoff Oberlin

Writing for Money
Working at Home While the Kids Are There, Too
Surviving Separation and Divorce
The Angry Child (co-written with Dr. Tim Murphy)
The Insider's Guide to Pittsburgh (collaboration)
The Everything American History Book

Writing for Quick Cash

Turn Your Way with Words into Real Money

Loriann Hoff Oberlin

AMACOM

American Management Association

New York • Atlanta • Brussels • Chicago • Mexico City • San Francisco
Shanghai • Tokyo • Toronto • Washington, D.C.

Special discounts on bulk quantities of AMACOM books are available to corporations, professional associations, and other organizations. For details, contact Special Sales Department, AMACOM, a division of American Management Association, 1601 Broadway, New York, NY 10019.
Tel.: 212-903-8316. Fax: 212-903-8083.
Web site: www.amacombooks.org

This publication is designed to provide accurate and authoritative information in regard to the subject matter covered. It is sold with the understanding that neither the publisher nor the author is engaged in rendering legal, accounting, or other professional service. If legal advice or other expert assistance is required, the services of a competent professional person should be sought.

Various names used by companies to distinguish their software and other products can be claimed as trademarks. AMACOM uses such names throughout this book for editorial purposes only, with no intention of trademark violation. All such software or product names are in initial capital letters or ALL CAPITAL letters. Individual companies should be contacted for complete information regarding trademarks and registration.

Library of Congress Cataloging-in-Publication Data

Oberlin, Loriann Hoff, 1961–
    Writing for quick cash : turn your way with words into real money / Loriann Hoff Oberlin.
        p.   cm.
    Includes bibliographical references and index.
    ISBN-10 0-8144-7199-4 (pbk.)
    ISBN-13 978-0-8144-7199-9
    1. Authorship—Marketing.   2. Authorship.   I. Title.

PN161.O34   2003
808'.02'023—dc21   2003014711

Printing number

10   9   8   7   6   5   4   3

To my parents, Elmer and Mary Jane Hoff, who fostered my curiosity

and talent. To my children, Andy and Alex, who inspire me every day.

And to my husband, Bob, who lives the writing life lovingly by my side.

Annotated Table
of Contents

Where is the work? How has the writing world changed in a
new economy? This chapter shows you the money, encourages
you, and gives you tips and gift suggestions to support you on
your freelance journey.

The well-connected writer needs assistance purchasing the
proper computer, furniture, and reference books. Tips on copyright, legal questions, taxes, home offices, and how to boost
your profits are included.

Writers love to ask questions. Learn how to satisfy your curiosity, conduct interviews, and weave your facts into convincing copy that leads to sales. If you never took a journalism
class—or even if you did—this chapter has all you need to
craft leads, weed out unnecessary words, and write tight.

Cash in on comedy, tempt your readers' taste buds, or break into a publication writing filler material. You may even have the background for encyclopedia and reference writing. If you build a reputation with smaller items, you can earn quick cash and open editorial doors.

Selling your sentiments and poetry to the greeting card industry brightens someone's day and adds income to your bank account. Here is how to study the market and approach editors.

How do you market your great idea to a magazine or newspaper? It starts with studying the markets and writing a convincing query letter. This chapter also discusses how to reslant published material for future sales, and how to break into the trade journal market as well.

The right combination of journalistic savvy, professional etiquette, and photographic skill can be your passport to further feature articles as well as more successful public relations work. Learn how to obtain stock photography and select necessary equipment, too.

Share your knowledge and relate your own experiences by setting up courses, running successful seminars, or speaking before groups. This chapter explores various teaching situations, including distance learning. Proofreading, copyediting, and indexing are all specialized opportunities affording additional income.

Acknowledgments

OF ALL THE BOOKS AND ARTICLES I'VE WRITTEN, IT SEEMS THAT THE topic of writing resonates most with readers. I've received correspondence and e-mails from writers of all ages, from various walks of life, and with diverse goals. Obviously, there is a huge pool of untapped talent out there, and many writers venturing down the publishing path. For that reason, I'm thrilled that Ellen Kadin and AMACOM Books recognized the value in this project and worked with me to bring this advice to aspiring and experienced writers alike.

My thanks to everyone at AMACOM Books for shepherding this project into print. Certainly, my former students and avid readers of my work have inspired me with great questions that I researched and included in this text. I also appreciate the insights of fellow communicators and editors including Gary Alt, Jackie Barrett-Hirschhaut, Sandra Louden, Gail Martin, Debbie Neveleff, Mary Jo Rulnick, and Syl Sobel.

Of course, my family deserves some applause. My sons, Andy and Alex, endure my long stretches at the keyboard, often without complaint, and they pay me the ultimate compliment when they allow me to become editor of their own projects! My husband, Bob, makes the writing life easier, fun filled, and much less solitary. Thanks, guys, for your support!

—Loriann Hoff Oberlin

Writing for
Quick Cash

Introduction

SO YOU WANT TO BE A WRITER? CONGRATULATIONS! YOU'VE TAKEN
that first step by acknowledging your passion for print. As I've learned
through years of teaching and public speaking, there are thousands of
closet writers among us. They find themselves in all lines of work, in
many neighborhoods, and with varying degrees of talent. It doesn't
matter whether these aspiring writers are young or old, male or female, wealthy or just getting by. Experience tells me that there are
thousands—maybe millions—of people wanting to get published.
You're one of them, no doubt, if you opened this book. Some of the
most enthusiastic writers are young people.

What does it take to make your writing sell, especially during an
economic downturn? Higher education isn't always necessary, but
degrees do matter for professionals who write books and articles. You
can use your education and years of experience to garner better writing assignments and publishing opportunities. But lack of education
does *not* necessarily mean closed publishing doors. For most of us,
the determining factor is the quality of our work and where we've
been published. So start now, even if it's a not-so-wonderful economy. The more you write, the better a writer you'll become. The more
you pitch editors or clients, the more convincing those pitches will become. Eventually, you'll see results.

For certainly, we writers are an eclectic group. The main difference, however, between those writers who see their names in print
and those who hide their work in desk drawers comes down to action.

1

It is whether you can create good material and successfully sell it. This book will help you to accomplish both tasks—to write well *and* to sell—in addition to inspiring you with ideas.

As I tell my writing students and those I meet at conferences, I am living proof that you can become a writer. You can make quick cash, and advance your interests. Of course, if I encounter aspiring writers who think the publishing path equates to the instant lottery, I politely correct them because advancement takes diligence. Accept that you must sacrifice leisure time in order to succeed. Accept also that the publishing business operates at a far slower pace than we might like.

Actually, these facts—that you can have fun and make money albeit with some patience—don't surprise many people. What causes their eyes to startle is my telling them that almost *anyone* can be a successful writer, provided the person has a passion for writing and at least a modicum of talent.

How can that be? How can an ordinary Joe or Jane compete with writers whose bylines appear in glossy magazines or on the spines of bookstore titles? How can it be, especially if Joe or Jane holds a day job, and has only a few hours each week to spend at the keyboard?

Every person has a learning curve about some subject. That is, you know more about something than your friend, the guy down the street, or the person who lives across the country. In fact, a novice might actually have an easier time getting published with an article idea than I might, even though I'm several rungs ahead of the person on the writing ladder (at least for the moment). When approaching editors, the nurse and the certified financial planner have credibility and clout when they use R.N. or C.F.P. after their names. Yes, I've also contributed to health and financial pages in my freelance career, even though I don't hold any medical degree, and I'm certainly not an accountant or a certified financial planner.

There is a reason behind the mantra "write what you know." Credentials are handy sales tools. Since writers frequently hear the admonition "don't give up your day job," it's refreshing to learn that you don't have to—or perhaps shouldn't—at least for now.

Take the student of mine who was a baker at a grocery store. She was a little unsure that she belonged in my class after we'd all introduced ourselves, and the students had spoken of their goals. She almost dropped out until I said, "Of course you have something to offer.

Tons of editors need holiday baking tips or kid-party ideas for parents." She left that day with six different article and filler ideas, and indeed she stayed the course—literally! Like this woman, you also know something that others yearn for—knowledge, firsthand experience, insight, or opinion.

Whether you write about what you know or branch out to other topics, your writing can lead to further opportunities or, indeed, to a brand-new career. When I began freelancing, I never thought I'd write books, merely magazine and newspaper articles, press releases, and collateral copy. Obviously, I underestimated my own talent, because *Writing for Quick Cash* is my seventh book.

As you read this book, expect to alter your writing goals. By the time you close the cover, you'll have more ideas than you do now as you read this introduction, for the opportunities I present will spark ideas. If this book doesn't in some way boost your productivity or your professional image, perhaps yielding a few more sales if you're self-employed, I'd be very surprised. Best case: You'll do many of these things, plus enjoy some new—and fun—writing avenues. This book shows you how to use creative energies you never knew you had. With those expanded horizons, sometimes you may choose a new path and sometimes new material will seem to find you.

You may decide to begin as a part-timer and perhaps later make the leap to full-time writing. Rest assured, there is a place for you in the world of print. We live in an information-driven society. We want our news instantly. We want research that succinctly shows us how to become healthier, wealthier, wiser, more successful, more popular, or just plain happier. And we yearn for new opinions and different insights. Depending on your qualifications, your talent, the time you can devote to the craft of writing, and plain old luck, your publishing road may be a high-speed expressway to success, or you may need to traverse a few rough spots and learn to cope with shifts in the economy.

Writing can also help smooth professional turbulence. My co-author of *The Angry Child,* Dr. Tim Murphy, spent more than two decades as a practicing psychologist before becoming a state senator and now a member of Congress. He contributed articles and always gave interviews when requested. He shared with me that one way psychologists could survive challenging economic times is by keeping their names in print. When families needed counseling or educational testing, whom do you think they thought of first? Indeed when our book was published, it gave Dr. Murphy's advice and professional insights a brand-new, highly rewarding forum that reached millions.

I can assure you—if you don't choose to write about your vocation, your interests, your expertise, or even your favorite vacation spot, someone else will. So let that writer be you, and reap the rewards of recognition, possible job promotions, income advantages, and a few of the other perks of the writing life, along the way.

CHAPTER 1

A World of Opportunities

ANYONE CAN CALL HIMSELF OR HERSELF A WRITER. MANY PEOPLE DO. They write for fun, cathartic release, or the pure love of words. But when someone else—particularly with praise or remuneration in hand—calls you a writer, that is when you know that you truly are one.

If you write for pleasure, this book provides dozen of opportunities to turn that pleasure into profit. Some may be hidden, but they're out there. I remember as a college senior getting ready to test the job-search waters.

"Are you sure you want to be a writer?" the placement director asked. I can still remember the serious tone conveyed, as if perhaps I was committing myself to a path I'd later regret. I accepted then that this man, charged with guiding job applicants, was asking tough questions—necessary when navigating from collegiate life to the competitive business landscape—to inject a dose of reality. Never to be daunted by challenging odds, I persisted.

Just a few years into my writing journey, I opened my mail to find a friendly note. This same man had spotted my byline in the slick, glossy pages of an airline magazine. He clipped out the article and scrawled on it how proud he was to see my accomplishments. It was the first of many clippings he would send my way until, I can only assume, the novelty of seeing my name in print wore off. Nonetheless, I knew I had made it.

My path to publishing, having begun in the mid-1980s recession, was a slow and steady climb. I started with small projects at often tinier publications. The checks paid for two tanks of gas back then—and probably only one tank today. I also started in what you'd colloquially call a moonlighting capacity since I had a day job, but one that didn't fully showcase my writing talents. When interviewed, I've often described writing as the one form of moonlighting the boss is least likely to resist. Think about it. If you announce you're going to the local retail store to work from 6 to 10 P.M., you might spawn questions of how awake you'll be the next day or whether your other boss is getting your best efforts. Announce, though, that you're going home to put the finishing touches on a magazine manuscript, and you'll likely elicit questions such as "Really? How did you get that assignment?" or "When does that come out?" I'm not certain why, except that writing carries a certain cachet that impresses people. Perhaps because many try, many more give up, and only a few hearty souls succeed. It leaves people with a positive impression, not a threatening one.

Writing in the evenings also gave me a creative outlet. In time, I cut back my hours on the day job and freelanced full-time. Through advertising copy, newspaper, and magazine features; public relations (PR) work; special event promotion; teaching; and greeting card and filler submissions, I made contacts, but more important, I grew tremendously as a writer. I not only polished my skills but my inquisitive nature blossomed, no doubt aided by steady work, public recognition, and ultimately, a new title of "author." Learning to write a book proposal was by far the career turner, for more than half a dozen have turned into books that have been granted that coveted place in the library card catalog and bookstore database. You will also meet success if you persevere on your own publishing path.

The 1990s and New Horizons

Although a recession ushered in the 1990s, opportunities for freelancers and corporate communicators increased at a healthy pace by the mid-decade mark. One reason can be expressed in two words: the Internet. Suddenly, everyone was trying this new medium. Either the Internet or the World Wide Web became crucial to your work each day, or by night curiosity got the better of you. Popular online services made browsing a form of entertainment. A world of information lay at a person's fingertips—literally—with the click of a mouse. Though technology had changed, the age-old caveat guiding writers had not. Wherever there is information flow, so too will there be writers.

Those wielding their pens or prolific at the keyboard have distinct advantages in some geographic areas. Technical writers fare well in high-tech corridors such as Boston, Seattle, northern California, and northern Virginia. New York City boasts the most plentiful publishing opportunities because it is the center of the industry, and many editors by day turn freelancer by evening. Washington, D.C., which is home to government, professional organizations, and leading health-care research, also attracts writers. Trade journals abound in the District, as do opportunities to write proposals, grants, manuals, and public relations material. Major universities across the country often have their own publishing operations, creating additional writing and research positions.

If you don't live in one of these hot markets, don't dismay. It may take a bit more time to become noticed, but technology is on your side when it comes to working at a distance. If millennium madness and Y2K fears kept computer jobs in hot demand, the Internet and telecommuting trends gave a financial boost to writers, at least until the next blip on the radar screen.

The Changing Face of Publishing

As the decade ended, traditional print publishers faced competition for the leisure dollar. According to the Newspaper Association of America, newspaper circulation figures, on average, shrank in the 1990s because of television, the Internet, and even price hikes for the daily or Sunday editions. Only the largest newspapers with circulations of more than 500,000 showed gains, among them the *New York Daily News, Chicago Tribune, Los Angeles Times, Newsday,* the *New York Times,* the *Washington Post*, and *USA Today*. New and different means of obtaining information benefited some while jeopardizing others. Book sales faired well, with a slight increase between 2000 and 2001. Some magazines, however, closed their doors because they couldn't retain readers and found the advertising climate growing softer still. Still others went from six issues per year to quarterly publication.

One publisher bought another. Mass conglomeration pushed the need for profits even higher, and many lesser-known authors felt at a disadvantage because bigger-name talent garnered better publicity, sales, and led to the better bottom lines. Series publishing became the focus of publisher lists as well (for example the Dummies books). Readers were guaranteed a "brand" and publishers often kept profits in-house by offering work-for-hire rather than royalty-based contracts. It was a competitive market, yet still one that showcased the diverse talents of many well-known and lesser-established writers.

Then came September 11, 2001. One wouldn't ordinarily link publishing perils to a terrorist attack, but then again, nothing of this magnitude had ever transpired. Since some time has elapsed, let me chronicle the domino effect these assaults had on the publishing industry.

Terrorist attacks led to recession fears and belt-tightening. Lost jobs gave way to less disposable income, which, of course, meant softer book and magazine sales. As companies had fewer advertising dollars, magazines shrank in size, causing a glut of unused, already purchased editorial material. Freelance freezes were common. Add in another wild card—anthrax, whether real or the threat thereof.

Many media outlets found themselves in a tenuous spot. Traditional print media determine a sale or uncover the next great idea in piles of paper and published clips. Though e-submissions are sometimes feasible, fears of computer viruses make many editors think twice before clicking on an attached file. Suddenly, the slush pile—that not-so-enviable spot that occasionally yields a bestseller or prime feature writer—became more than an eyesore, but acquired even more dreaded status in the wake of anthrax assaults.

Publishers took aggressive, but perfectly understandable precautions. Steven Zeitchik, reporting in the online newsletter of *Publisher's Weekly*, wrote that "[the *New Yorker*] won't open any package that doesn't come by UPS or FedEx, a policy intended not only to protect the magazine from terrorists but from the accidental contamination of mail that moves through the post office's general pool." Meanwhile, as anthrax fears intensified, several publishers tightened their policies. Because some large houses had never accepted unsolicited manuscripts, they surely wouldn't be opening them in this fearful climate. Furthermore, mail not addressed to a specific individual would be returned. "Unknowns" had an especially tough task. How were writers to get through the gate? Mystery authors and their packages got nowhere fast. This might have been a boost to literary agents, who serve as a first screen for manuscripts. Those authors without agents may have recognized a need for one. Overall, everyone in the industry saw some level of fallout. Even seasoned veterans who had once worked as magazine staffers faltered as freelancers.

Lost Cause or Hope Found?

"What great odds, Loriann," you must be thinking. "If seasoned pros face competition, what about me?" There is hope. If writing is your profession or necessary to career progression; or a hobby; or, dare I say, a passion, I'm here only to encourage you. Twenty years and more than half-a-dozen book titles have taught me to weather the dry spells. So can you. No industry is immune to tough economies. We don't have to look beyond the Enron debacle to see how a prestigious accounting firm with once secure positions suffered. If you're looking for guarantees and an easy path to profit, my guess is you'll still be searching long after reading this book.

Change requires regrouping. The effect of this new economy is that you'll need to be even more professional and, at times, more patient and understanding, particularly in regard to submitting material. You may need to go the extra mile in selling yourself and making contacts to ensure your material lands in welcome hands. Statistics are on your side.

According to the *2002–03 Occupational Outlook Handbook,* published by the Bureau of Labor Statistics at the U.S. Department of Labor, employment of writers and editors is expected to increase faster than average for all occupations (21 to 35 percent) through the year 2010. Periodicals, online publications, and the demand for technical writing are responsible for this optimism. Advertising, public relations, and specialty writing (medical, legal, and technical) are expected to grow. Despite terrorist attacks that spiraled a slowdown in certain businesses, other industries received an unexpected economic boost, among them defense contractors; security-technology firms; and, surprisingly, housing (made more affordable with slashed interest rates). Where there is adversity, there also lies opportunity— and the savvy writer looks for those niches.

Encouragement Found

Just as I saved my college placement director's notes to me, you, too, can build an encouragement file filled with a copy of that first check, your first published clip, or any item that lends a smile. Trust me; there will be days when you need the pick-me-up. Freelancing is often isolating. For that reason, hang around positive people who believe in your goals. Writer's conferences are, by far, one of the best places to find other creative types and to be filled with their infectious spirit of wanting to get published. It never fails when I attend such a conference that I leave with renewed goals, a hefty dose of validation, and probably some surprise element I never dreamed of receiving, maybe a chance meeting with an agent, a collaborator, who knows. Surround yourself with encourage-ment right from the start.

Survival Strategies in the New Economy

Culled from my classroom and online lectures, I will share with you a list of writer's traits. If for no other reason than to declare yourself normal, use these for validation or inspiration. For starters, writers must be deadline oriented and well organized, and have the ability to take notes and absorb detail. Above all, they must take their writing seriously. I've never met a writer who wasn't an avid reader. As Stephen King writes in his book *On Writing: A Memoir of the Craft,* "Reading is the creative center of a writer's life." Sure is! Thus, the love of bookstores, newsstands, and libraries demands little explana-tion. Your loved ones know what I mean if you suddenly disappear in a crowd. The surest place to find a writer is that magazine stand or turnaround stile of paperback books. We writers seem to automati-cally gravitate to the written word. Like Stephen King, get into the habit of carrying a book with you for idle moments, and crack the covers before opting for TV.

If you haven't yet become friends with your local librarian, do so today. I've found the expertise of a good reference librarian to be invaluable, and I've also found some new markets and magazines in library periodical rooms or on newsstands.

Clipping, filing, and thinking—what I call the constant pursuits of any writer—will be sparks to your inner muse. In a tough economy, they'll also be your salvation, for without a healthy imagination, you can forget it. A writer is what he or she perceives on a future page. Finally, this path requires discipline, patience, and tenacity. You will face occasional rejection, and you'll probably want to argue the merits of your work. Don't. You may need the good wishes or referral of that editor someday. He or she could move to another publication as well, so swallow this temptation and try to learn from constructive criticism. Using that discipline, patience, and tenacity, try to write every day, even when it means doing a complete rewrite. There will be moments when it seems like a chore, but the more you commit pen to paper (or fingers to keyboard), the better writer you'll become. As one freelancer imparted to me, nothing replaces parking your butt in the chair and just doing it. On those days when you simply can't muster the time (let's hope those days are few) or sorely lack the motivation to write, there is usually something you can do to propel your writing vision forward. It could be assembling your clips, making follow-up telephone calls, or researching your next project. These tasks, however mundane, steer you and your ideas toward acceptance.

Of practical concern, you'll want to be extra vigilant in presenting your work. Always send it to a real, living, breathing person—no "Dear Editors" or "To Whom It May Concern." Always identify yourself on each page and by return address. In normal or in hypersensitive times, submit clean work with a minimum of tape. If you must purchase new packing material, that is the price to pay for being a freelance writer. Postage should be affixed straight and mailing labels should be legible. Anything hastily assembled might become a big red flag.

Whenever possible, you should alert recipients to an in-bound package, and follow the publisher's guidelines, which are readily available on Web sites and in resource books. Thus, ignorance is no excuse. Get a stamp made that reads "requested material." Especially when stamped in red, it lends added clout to mailings, helping them past the gatekeeper. Of course, use this approach only when you have indeed made personal contact and been given the go-ahead.

Timing is also imperative. No, timing is really everything! To match the right idea with the right publisher, you must develop a keen sense of submission timing. How many writers have lamented hearing the words, "Oh, we ran that six months ago," or "We're on deadline, check back with us." All editors demand solid ideas and timely material. Our challenge as idea suppliers is spotting what the public wants or needs to read, only ahead of time.

Trend Setting and Idea Catching

So how do we spot trends and combine awareness with the six-month-plus lead time—or, in the case of books, two-year lead time—that it takes to see print? Thankfully, we live in a not-so-shy world where medical breakthroughs, technological advances, and product announcements are shared. These tip the savvy writer to a story, filler, or book waiting to be written. PR practitioners live for the eager journalist willing to scour press releases. Use sources such as PartyLine or Profnet to connect with account executives who are disseminating plentiful information.

Events listed on public calendars give a writer the heads-up. The opening of the museum exhibit in Washington, D.C., featuring the White House clothing of Jacqueline Kennedy brought a raison d'être to discuss Camelot once more. In fact, *Washington Post* reporters seized the opportunity to feature Georgetown walking tours with Mrs. Kennedy's favorite haunts. The Olympic Games give the savvy reporter a chance to write personality profiles and inspirational stories of current athletes, even those medal winners from decades ago. Examples of other scheduled events include major construction projects, sporting events, celebrity contract negotiations, income tax deadlines, trial dates, and holidays.

Statistics spark debate and revelation. *American Demographics* and *USA Today* are vital in bringing future trends to our attention. The astute writer will look at a *USA Today* Snapshots column and realize the fodder found. For instance, two snapshots depicted that facing a crowd isn't easy and that weddings cost the most in New York

City. Neither challenge is likely to dissipate soon. Ideas: speaking tips and how to have an elegant wedding on a budget. Newspaper as well as broadcast advertising clues us into current trends. Years ago, you didn't see as many advertisements for antianxiety medication and a host of other disorders. Sure, some of this is plain old marketing, but does the proliferation of prescription advertisements mean we're all struggling with mood management, stress, and personality disorders? A journalist digs a bit deeper.

Emerging technology hints at what lies ahead. Some topics, however, remain timeless. In the business, we call these evergreens. It's that service orientation that editors strive for, and writers should ingrain into their souls—anything that makes the reader healthier, wealthier, wiser, more popular, or better adjusted. Just like the wedding and speaking challenges, other examples include back-to-school shopping and how to survive the holidays. Add a new spin on an otherwise overdone topic, and look for the not-so-obvious angles. On the anniversary coverage of 9/11, one network reporter interviewed twins who had lost their twin brother or sister when the Twin Towers fell. It was a unique and poignant angle that made that network's coverage stand apart from the obvious.

Converting Dormant Clients Through Promotion

There is no such thing as a former client. A dormant client, yes, but there is always tomorrow's sales opportunity!

Whether you're a seasoned pro or just building a list of writing clients, take every available opportunity to market your writing services. If you're in a down cycle because editors or clients haven't been calling, take a fresh look at the business profile you're marketing by revisiting your stationery, business cards, even the signature closing your e-mails. No company can hire you if the key decision makers don't know you exist or aren't aware of your skills. And please, do not use quill pens as your graphic symbol on business cards because this is the telltale sign of a beginner. Try to market yourself as you wish to be perceived, as either the generalist or specialist you are. Design different cards if necessary, and consider a Web presence for those who might look for your services on the Internet.

A job well done keeps clients calling. I can't tell you how many referrals I have received over the years because my name topped people's lists of available, hard-working writers. There have been projects I've had to turn down and refer to other writers.

Word of mouth begins with yours. Tell everyone you're a writer. Boost referrals by mailing or e-mailing dormant or prospective clients. Keep these key people abreast of your news clippings, speeches, book or article publicity, TV or radio interviews, and, if you're truly creative, send them a briefing—a newsletter of sorts, at least semiannually. If invitations to speak before community, library, or bookstore groups don't come to you, solicit them. Many groups won't have budgets, so be prepared to speak gratis, simply for the promotional value. Remember to keep track of how much time you give away freely (that could be billable time). Write the introduction for any hosts introducing you. With every submission to a commercial publisher, craft your own bio. Don't leave even two or three sentences to chance. Control what image you present.

Share feedback. Betsy Lerner, in *The Forest for the Trees: An Editor's Advice to Writers,* writes, "No matter how great a person is, in America we still prefer to have greatness conferred by others." If someone compliments your magazine or newspaper work, ask the person to write a favorable letter to the editor praising the piece.

For years, I've gone out of my way to thank key career contacts because the words "please" and "thank you" are seldom used in the business climate. When they are, you'll see their impact. I once thanked an editor for taking a chance on me knowing she already had a stable of writers. She was amazed, and I solidified a deeper, positive impression.

The 80/20 rule applies to all businesspeople, including writers. You will find that 80 percent of your business comes from 20 percent of your clients (editors, too). So keep those folks happy. It's great to have not only the income but also the routine of working with the same clients. The convenience has a flip side, of course. Lose two clients and that's substantial.

Diversification and writing for new markets can help writers to survive a tough economy. The more markets or editors you query, the better your odds of always having steady work. When you've successfully completed a job, ask satisfied clients for their endorsement, even if it's a quick e-mail applauding you. Ask for quantified results. For instance, if your clients can say that sales of their products improved by X percent, largely because of a marketing publication you designed, that is concrete and convincing evidence.

Resist the notion that people will pronounce you a braggart if you self-promote. Done with a bit of savvy and common sense, sending along appropriate material usually conveys concern for your client, a willingness to work together again, and healthy self-confidence. If you don't believe in your efforts, don't expect others to either. Most businesspeople respect a go-getting, can-do attitude. Every purchase and every satisfied reader or client counts for those of us who derive our living from the published word. Proper promotion also keeps rejection and down cycles in perspective.

Writer's Conferences

Writer's conferences provide outstanding opportunities to network. Even if you aren't a featured speaker, you can participate in panel discussions and ask insightful questions. Lower attendance costs by volunteering to work the registration table, sharing a room with another writer, and registering in advance. Don't forget to dress for first impressions. I'm amazed at how participants attend conferences in blue jeans and tennis shoes. I attended my first conference in a blue suit and blouse, carried a slender brief case, and handed out cards sealed in my engraved card case. Maybe I went too far, but at the networking lunch, one of the two agents at the conference sat down next to me. The agent later approached me about a project she had in mind. I'm not implying that looks alone help you sell your work, but if I were an agent or editor, a professional appearance would help me to size up which writers I wanted to work with.

Seven Big Mistakes in Trying to Attract Work

1. *Sounding Desperate.* Forget lines such as "I've got the time to work on extra projects." Focus instead on how your work will benefit them.

2. *Inundating Editors or Prospective Clients with Too Many Clips or Writing Samples.* Three to five should suffice. If your client is nearby, schedule a face-to-face meeting to review your portfolio. Excess materials are likely to meet the circular file.

3. *Acknowledging Your Beginner Status.* When prospecting a client, this is *not* the time to reveal, "I've never done this before, just give me the chance." Instead of going after a high-circulation, glossy magazine that millions of other writers are vying for, set the bar a little lower for quicker cash and success. If it's a client job, as long as it's not too far a stretch, there are always resources if you need help with the project.

4. *Showing Ignorance of Schedule and Protocol.* Don't expect a newspaper editor to return your self-addressed, stamped envelope (SASE). It just isn't going to happen. All editors are harried; those on daily deadlines even more so. Book editors must garner the support of colleagues on the editorial board. Greeting card editors also ask for input.

5. *Speaking Poorly of Former Clients or Editors.* You never know who knows whom in this industry. Bad-mouthing anyone simply isn't worth the risk.

6. *Writing Everything on Speculation (on Spec).* Beginning writers find themselves in the proverbial catch-22. How do they get published without clips? How do they get clips without having been published before? If a writer submits on spec, it's easy to view the submission as a finished cast-in-stone piece. Querying (discussed in Chapter 6) is the preferred route for most publishers. An exception is that greeting cards, fillers, hints, humor, or fiction must be judged in their complete form. Book proposals that contain a sample chapter stand a better chance of landing a contract, unless there is a comprehensive record of past projects.

7. *Letting on That You Write Part-Time.* I'd keep it quiet unless you must reveal the fact. Some editors enjoy knowing you're there at a moment's notice. If you divulge your limited schedule, your editor might seek services elsewhere. Part-timers should focus on projects that don't require a wealth of research, subscribe to online library services, use e-mail and faxes for interviews, and perhaps even ask permission of their employers (if you write for another publication, you may need to obtain clearance to freelance).

A Head Start

If you're afraid that your full-time success will be confounded by your part-time status, give yourself a head start out of the gate. Do some research and organize your thoughts in an action plan.

This might mean devoting two to six months to reading appropriate resources or taking an evening or online class.

Building a library of helpful resources or spending time at a public library lends another advantage. Every writer should have access to *Writer's Market, The Writer's Handbook, The Writer's Guide to Book Editors, Publishers and Literary Agents* (for book authors), and *Literary Market Place* (though because of price, check out your library's holdings).

Internet access is a necessity, though ever since a writing student asked me if all material had to be typewritten before submission, I quickly learned not to assume any prior knowledge. (The answer there was yes, by the way!) The same must-have list includes the most up-to-date dictionary and thesaurus along with *The Elements of Style.* Yes, this means ditching that 1970s or 1980s dictionary, for you can be sure your editors use the most current resources. You should too. Also, decide upon a stylebook for your writing focus. Some publishers or employers have their own style guidelines or use some of the style manuals listed in Chapter 3.

Choices Ahead

Decide which markets, editors, or clients you'll prospect first. Where will you put your efforts to get published and be paid as quickly as possible? Subsequent chapters help guide your decisions, so temporarily postponing your final publishing plan is wise until you finish this book.

All writers wake at odd hours wondering if they made the right decisions, sometimes haunted by the notion that they could have done themselves one better in any given contract, negotiation, or deal. Don't go there. At the very least, resist going there too frequently.

You'll learn better survival skills and business tactics as you develop your own writing style. When setting rates, let the economy

Encouraging Young Writers

Although this book is geared toward adult writers, just about everything I say applies to young talent as well. And if you're a young writer, I commend you. If I had the courage to submit my work at a younger age, and to really study first how to do that in a professional manner, I would be farther down the publishing path.

Many teens and college students seek part-time jobs and credentials to enhance their résumés. Writing is one of those endeavors. Just as I advise adults to hold onto their day jobs, I'm not telling you to ignore working as a lifeguard, baby-sitter, or retail clerk. I am telling young people that writing could lead to further income, for college or any other goal. Besides, it impresses teachers.

Parents and educators can encourage children by asking them to write letters to their favorite celebrities, sports stars, or politicians as well as letters to the editor when they're old enough. Kids can create invitations, family newsletters, or write for their school's publications. Nothing replaces an old-fashioned notebook or journal. Consult my software recommendations and the Appendix for appropriate resources.

and your experience guide you, as well as the market where you reside and work. If you set the pay scale too high, you may snag few assignments. Set the bar too low, and you'll risk working numerous hours well below minimum wage. You might get frustrated and be tempted to quit. Charging a fair rate enlightens clients that you're a professional, not a clerk. It also gives you the opportunity to do excellent work and build higher-paying assignments into your future repertoire.

Consult resources such as *Writer's Market, The Writer's Market Companion,* and *National Writers Union Guide to Freelance Rates & Standard Practices* or browse writing Web sites and newsgroups to ask what others believe are fair rates, given your circumstances and geography. Another source of current salary and freelance pay rates are writing organizations such as the Author's Guild or the Society for Technical Communicators (STC).

At magazine and book publishers, beginning writers are wise to write more, negotiate less. Once you've proved your worth or have a hefty trail of clips, you're certainly within your rights to ask for an increase or refuse to settle at the first offer. Some ask, and rightly so, what we're looking at in terms of potential income. According to the Bureau of Labor Statistics, the median annual earnings for salaried writers and authors were $42,270 in 2000 ($47,790 for technical writers).

If you freelance for newspapers and magazines, a few local publications, and commercial clients, you can realistically gross $25,000 to $35,000 (expenses may yield a lower net income). To gross what your experienced comrades earn, hustle even harder; focus on national and trade magazines; book advances and royalties, teaching assignments, and for-profit clients; and consider a writing specialty (medical or technical writing). Many writers earn six-figure incomes as well.

Once you see your name in print, you're in a better position to specialize. This decision depends on your writing and financial goals. I've met plenty of writers who work in public relations and business or technical writing, while also contributing newspaper features or magazine travel articles. But I've also known beginning writers who only wanted to focus on greeting card writing—a task that requires very little overhead and where the writer could be in business in a few hours. Generally cast your net wide to as many editors and markets before reining in only a few. In a lagging economy, that advice has saved numerous writers from floundering.

Building a Portfolio of Samples and Clips

Clips (short for clippings or tear sheets) prove that you're a published writer. It's merely a publishing term for wonderful photocopies, with *wonderful* being the operative word. This is *not* where you slap any old clipping onto a photocopier and pray it comes out clear. Master the art of that machine. I've hung around the self-serve copy center of my local office supply store so often that I've been mistaken for staff some days, but I know how to make a good photocopy.

Always obtain at least one (hopefully a few) original copy of your published work. Be certain to keep the masthead, but if that's too large (such as a paper's lengthy masthead), find a smaller version inside the publication, along with a published date. As a writer, you should date everything you clip, even material for your research files. Have you ever referred to some earlier clipping and had no clue how dated the research was?

Paste the publication's masthead (even if not the main masthead but a smaller version inside the magazine or newspaper), and the publication date, along with your clipping onto a standard sheet of paper. If necessary, you'll need to reduce onto 8½-by-11-inch stock. If you don't have the masthead, simply type the publication's name and date. Use the photo, lightness, and darkness commands to help you master the art of photocopying. Neatness counts. Correction fluid helps to disguise any specks or lines that don't belong.

Published clips are paramount. They sell you. In most cases, you'll mail or fax them to your editor. Online clips (directing editors to Web sites where your work is published) can also be helpful. Still, it's best to build a file with several sets of clips just in case you need to put these into the mail quickly.

Occasionally you'll need a portfolio to present to clients. Place each original in clear sleeves for protection. Multiple originals give you one portfolio copy and one to manipulate on the photocopier. Section off the types of work your portfolio contains. Showing repeat work for the same clients creates an even more positive impression. As long as your portfolio doesn't shout school supply, you'll be in good shape. A professional-looking binder from an office supply store is fine.

Great Gift Suggestions for Writers

Even the most well-intentioned person can come up empty with gift ideas. Here's help:

- Subscriptions to writing magazines or daily newspapers for research
- Gift certificates to copy centers, office supply stores, or bookstores
- Fees for an online or continuing education or writer's conference (Hint: Maui is motivation!)
- Membership dues for a local or national writer's group
- Pens, paper, writing tablets, or virtually any desk accessory (Cross pens are great for signings)
- New computer, printer, peripheral, or software
- Fees for online research services such as elibrary.com
- New briefcase or personal CD player to tune out the world when writing
- Healthy snacks, gourmet coffees, herbal teas, or hot cocoa
- Homemade coupons for baby-sitting services or even dog walking so that the writer can do just that—write
- Siberian tiger to post as sentry at your office door!

CHAPTER 2

Organizing Yourself to Write

A WELL-CONNECTED WRITER HAS NOT ONLY THE RIGHT REFERENCE material but also the proper office configuration, furniture, equipment, and Internet connections. The pivotal word here is "proper," for poor ergonomics and faulty equipment lead to maladies such as carpal tunnel syndrome and, of course, that financial malady—lost income. In addition, writers need to know the essentials of copyright and libel, combined with a sharp professional look and time management skills, to become prolific. Ignore these factors and there could be some stumbling blocks ahead.

Home Offices

If you take your writing seriously, carve out a suitable home office. If you work out of employer-provided space, some of these techniques will also work for you.

The challenge of home offices is that invariably they are created with divergent goals—to integrate work and family life while at the same time to separate work from that life. Sometimes writers opt for one solitary spot; other times they create a dual-purpose space.

As writers, we are lucky that our craft melds so wonderfully with whatever we call home whether we reside in an efficiency apartment or a sprawling estate. Still, many writers view their workspace or lack of one as an impediment. Two caveats here: First, the space does not make you; your writing does. Second, this space in which you unleash your creativity today is likely to change, just as your life will, over the next three, five, or ten years. Those who start only with greeting cards could be in business by evening with the purchase of a typewriter as the bare minimum (though a computer is a wise purchase, especially with the advent of the Internet). Try writing books, however, with only an electric typewriter or submitting dot-matrix material to a glossy four-color magazine in Manhattan. As your career ambitions, skills, and potential markets expand, so too must your office and equipment.

When I began freelancing, home was a small two-bedroom garden apartment, and, literally, my writing life was scattered from the computer housed in the bedroom to my supplies tucked in a closet to my work that was either on or off the kitchen table. Upon moving into a house, I used the smallest bedroom as a home office until I moved two flights down to a finished basement. Finally, there was room for my burgeoning collection of books. Eight years later, I picked up once more, moving from Pennsylvania to Maryland. As realtors showed my fiancé and me new homes, they readily understood one important caveat: If it didn't have a space that could function as a home office, we didn't want to see it.

I share this story because I truly believe that our home offices don't need to compete for coverage in *Architectural Digest*. They just need to work. The same goes for computers and gadgetry. You don't need high-tech equipment, just appropriate tech.

Any Room Will Do

Survey your surroundings. Is there space not being used to its full potential? Don't be too particular, but pick a space with telephone jacks; several strategically placed electrical outlets; plenty of book-shelves; natural, fluorescent and incandescent light; enough space to grow your writing career; and, at the very best, a door. Look at every square foot of space—underneath the stairs and at the top of them, in corners of the kitchen, in sections of the garage, or in vacant but dreary spaces such as laundry or utility rooms. My job here isn't to incite home remodeling. Check out the Appendix for some resources, which if nothing more, will spark ideas if you have the luxury of cre-ating your home office from floorboard to ceiling. My own book

Working at Home While the Kids Are There, Too expands upon this discussion.

Important considerations are whether you have a family and how you like to work. If you require a separate entrance for clients, and you need the tax deduction, you must meet all IRS requirements. Do you need room for workers, additional equipment, or even a spouse or children working on the computer? Will you be comfortable in the space you deem ideal? When I moved to the basement, I immediately had more space, albeit it could get a bit chilly even with a sub-floor, carpeting, and insulation. What I found I'd taken for granted, but needed in daily doses, was sunlight. Basements or attics can rise to lofty status, but consider all ramifications, including the comfort factor, even the color of the walls. Research suggests that the color of a room can affect mood, so if you want to paint cream-colored walls a shade of blue for a placid and soothing effect, budget for this expenditure.

If you don't have a dedicated space—if you must continually clear the breakfast dishes to set up shop each morning—then so be it. You'll live. You'll work. You'll make the best of it.

Ergonomically Correct Furniture

You'll want furniture to be aesthetically pleasing and ergonomically correct. Government regulations have made most employers responsible for the ergonomic well-being of their employees, and while you might not expect a visit from the Occupational Safety & Health Administration (OSHA), I guarantee you'll care if you suffer aches and pains.

If you write at your desk, you'll want your writing surface to be generally 29 or 30 inches off the ground. However, if you will be typing, the surface height changes to 26 or 27 inches. And while older office furniture may be the right height, don't forget to measure the width. Today's computer monitors and keyboards require more room than yesterday's typewriters. You also want to be positioned so that your wrists are not bent in any direction, your head is tilted slightly down, your upper body remains straight, and there's no pressure at the back of your thighs. How prescient the advice that desk jobs can be a real pain!

Space-Saving Tips

Today, many people have great rooms, so they can convert a nook or cranny into a writing space. Purchase a screen or section off a room portion with an accordion door. Doors hide the stacks of creativity lurking within. Build desks and shelving into walls, or install recessed lights so that other fixtures don't take up valuable space.

Some writers living in small quarters turn to freestanding units (much like an armoire), which are available at furniture or office stores. These are often bare-bones accommodations, with room for computer equipment, a peripheral item, and a few supplies, but everything is in one spot.

By using lighter colors (off-white or pastel), you can make a small space feel much larger. Halogen and fluorescent bulbs produce more light, last longer, and use less energy. Task lighting is also efficient.

If you own two-drawer file cabinets, place a countertop slab atop these rather than investing in a desk that may or may not have adequate drawers. I prefer to have a set of hanging files immediately accessible, so I ordered furniture configured this way. When my children were younger, I had a separate cabinet that locked away business stationery, toner cartridges, and film. Building a cabinet high into a wall can achieve the same safety measures and free up much-needed floor space.

An adjustable chair is necessary, because the suggested height of your chair seat should be 15 to 21 inches from the floor. Someone else might sit in your chair, and the wrong chair height can lead to repetitive strain injuries. An improper chair will also cause back and circulatory problems, muscle aches, varicose veins, and swelling in the legs. Choose one of variable height with lower-back support.

Your feet should be either flat on the floor or flexed at a slight angle with some sort of footrest. Take frequent breaks in order to stretch and also to spark creativity. Workers who have back problems or other aches typically don't move around.

Carpal Tunnel Syndrome

Often considered to be a writer's ailment, carpal tunnel syndrome is a repetitive strain injury (RSI), the most common occupational condition of the computer era. It's caused by chronic compression of the median nerve as it passes through the wrist bones, which form a "tunnel" for the passage of tendons that flex the fingers and the median nerve. That compression can result in numbness, pain, burning, and tingling in the thumb, middle, and index fingers. It sometimes affects the wrist. Configure your body so that your wrists are not bent in any direction, especially not slanted uphill.

Any repetitive activity can cause these injuries, with or without typing. It's of concern to writers because we spend countless hours at our keyboards. Furthermore, if you fail to take breaks; work in high-pressure environments; have arthritis, diabetes, thyroid disease, or another serious medical condition, you're at risk of developing an RSI. Advanced age and weight gain place you at higher risk as well. If you're already suffering symptoms and find routine tasks painful, seek treatment immediately because the condition can be corrected with therapy and devices. Surgery is not the first line of treatment; prevention is. Set your keyboard so that you have your elbows at a 90-degree angle. You should not be reaching up or down in your lap. A keyboard drawer built into some computer workstations will achieve this. If a computer's mouse bothers you, try a trackball or wireless remote. Resist striking keys too forcefully. The resounding lesson here is to take breaks every ten to fifteen minutes to stretch.

Must-Have Equipment

The right telephone facilitates good communication. I'd recommend as many options as you can pack into one device at a reasonable price—two lines, speakerphone, automatic redial, a hold button, and call waiting (a service actually), as well as a mute button (to filter out Fido, the kids, or coworkers). Caller ID helps to screen calls. Voice mail often lets you check messages when offsite.

Fax machines have become affordable and commonplace. Purchase one only after you've made your computer and printer decisions because many printers are multifunction machines, and some computers have built-in fax modems. This I can assure you: Have fax, increase productivity. Miscellaneous equipment includes a calculator, music to drown out extraneous noise and keep you focused, and a tape recorder (and taping device for telephone interviews, used with permission of course). You must have backup storage. Burning your own CD backup is advisable because some data files won't fit onto traditional diskettes. Then there is the monster of all equipment decisions—your computer.

Computer and Printer Considerations

A computer will increase your profits, in most cases. Imagine retyping an entire page because you found one letter out of place. A computer increases your material's professional look. It saves you time. With time comes efficiency, and with efficiency comes increased profit. Don't be afraid to spend money for success, and don't be afraid to upgrade when the equipment you selected only a few years ago has become a technological dinosaur. If you don't have computer equipment, you will surely be competing against those who do.

It's your choice between the IBM-compatible personal computer and the Mac. I'm partial to the Mac because it was introduced when I began my career. Having said that, I've also used PCs. Your decisions must factor in what you already own, what systems your colleagues are on, not to mention price, discounts, and software. Always buy the maximum memory because new software eats this up faster than you can replace random access memory (RAM).

Printers must work with your system. Today, many people purchase a combination printer, fax, scanner, copier device. As a writer, you need high-quality text output. Opt for as many dots per inch as you can afford in resolution (laser printers have 1200 dpi). This creates a more pleasing presentation, and your editors will thank you for minimizing their eyestrain.

In fact, after you've read this book from cover to cover, try to predict the future of your writing life. If public relations, newsletter publishing, or self-publishing is in the offing, think seriously about a PostScript-compatible laser printer. PostScript is a page description language that desktop publishers use to create type that is similar to professional typesetting. This makes type in virtually any size, and thus having a large selection at your disposal gives you an added range of publishing possibilities. PostScript also enhances the look of graphics files imported into documents. PostScript printers aren't nearly as cost prohibitive as they were years ago. When choosing a printer, factor in the cost of replacement toner cartridges and other supplies.

Stocking Supplies

Not all supplies I list here will pertain to your type of writing, but you should consider stocking the following items:

- Blank cassette tapes
- Bookends
- A calendar or date book
- Computer disks or CD-RWs
- Correction fluid
- File folders
- Glue or rubber cement
- Index cards
- Large mailing envelopes or manuscript boxes
- Mailing labels
- Marking pens
- Notebooks (especially a portable kind)
- Padded envelopes
- Paper
- Paper clips
- Pencil sharpener
- Pens and pencils
- Postage stamps
- Reference books, especially an up-to-date dictionary and the-saurus
- A ruler and T-square
- Scissors
- Stapler, staples, and staple remover

- Sticky notes
- Storage boxes
- Tape (transparent and packaging varieties)
- Three-ring binders
- Typewriter ribbons or toner cartridges
- A typing stand

In addition, if you truly want to look professional, invest in stationery, matching envelopes, and business cards. By using Pagemaker software, I have saved money by designing my own camera-ready artwork. Whatever course you choose, make certain that it looks professional and that you've carried your design theme through on all printed matter.

If your services extend to photography, you should own a 35-mm camera and plenty of film. Allow for growth as your skills improve. This way you can add lenses, filters, and other equipment later. Newspaper work might necessitate a second camera for black-and-white photographs.

You can purchase most of your supplies at office superstores, supply outlets, direct-mail catalogs, or over the Internet. If you frequent an office supply store, sign up for its frequent customer card, earning you coupons and sometimes cash back.

Time Management for Writers

When people discover I'm an author, I sometimes get the impression that they think I lead a glamorous, relaxed work life. Okay, I've had my fifteen minutes of fame here and there, and I've enjoyed the flexibility that self-employment sometimes affords. What people don't see is that with these perks come isolation, little feedback on some days, and the very real temptation to do something else that takes care of the first two. Without developing a work plan and some discipline, your dream of a freelance career could become a nightmare of disorganization and goals not achieved.

In a 9-to-5 job, workers most likely have resources that include a receptionist, a secretary, an accounting department, marketing and PR specialists, planners, a personnel manager, and maybe even an in-house

Lower Expenses = Higher Income

Only you can create the proper balance between spending to make money and saving. Here are a few cost-cutting suggestions specifically geared toward writers:

- Ask suppliers or stores to offer you business discounts of at least 10 percent, and to allow this discount on top of advertised specials. If you teach or take classes, ask for educational discounts.

- Check the classifieds for gently used equipment, furniture, estate pieces, auctions, secondhand stores, warehouse clubs, and garage or moving sales. Proceed with caution when purchasing anything electronic or delicate (such as camera equipment).

- Building your own furniture or ordering unfinished pieces also saves money. Never pay full price for furniture in a retail showroom. Floor models and remnants might suit you fine.

- Use the time-zone advantage. East Coast writers can make West Coast calls and faxes after the close of business. West Coast writers should invest in phone cards because the rates beat some calling plans. Reach East Coast sources before you depart for any day job.

- Mail packages checked second-day service on the slip. I've had packages marked this way arrive overnight without paying for that service.

- Use self-addressed stamped postcards. You save on the stamp and envelope, and most editors reply faster when you provide check-off options.

- Use e-mail, if your editor approves, to send finished manuscripts, clips, or other requested material.

- Prepare your own taxes by using one of the many software packages such as TurboTax.

ℇ Don't give out cell phone numbers indiscriminately because you'll pay for someone else's convenience. Use toll-
free numbers.

ℇ Purchase office supplies in September when items are marked
down after the back-to-school rush.

ℇ Barter services with a vendor when you can strike a mutually
agreeable arrangement.

ℇ Add an endorsement onto your homeowner's policy if you
need business coverage but lack enough business income to
justify a separate policy.

print shop. If you're self-employed, you've said good-bye to those support functions. Put another way, you've added all these tasks plus trash
detail, too.

The problem is, if you're like me, you *are* tempted to take out the
garbage, fold the laundry, or unload the dishwasher—because, well,
the tasks are there, and you like to get things done. That is why
you're self-employed. Your best bet is to set regular hours and to
stick to them.

In order to become prolific, not to mention skilled, you must write
every day. Choose the time that is best for you. It might be first thing
in the morning when you feel freshest. It could be in the afternoon. It
could be in the evening after a day's work, or it could be after the kids
are in bed and the rest of the world is quiet. Just stick to your goal of
writing every day.

When not plying words, you can still effect your goals by doing
something writing related, such as research, photocopying clips, or
reading. No time? Too busy? We're all too busy with other things, but
we're all going to get older next year with or without having published
something (or several new things). If achieving your writing goals is
important to you, set aside the time. Break your work into manageable
segments, yielding a better work/life balance.

Enlisting family support truly helps. If those you love and live with
support your goals, it gives you needed cheerleading. Be honest about
your goals and how important your writing is to you. One student told

me that her husband was skeptical of her coming to class, investing the money in resources and magazines, and sending out several weeks' worth of submissions until she got her first acceptance, followed by her second, and then third. This husband surprised her with my first writing book as a Christmas present. Talk about the gift that says "I believe in you, honey!" My point is that you can't possibly do everything with perfection. Pick and choose, set boundaries, ask for help when you need it, and declare your right to pursue an important goal. Set some new time guidelines for yourself, and with your loved ones' help, for the family. Stick to it for six months and adjust the plan as needed.

Overcoming Other Obstacles

Stuck in the idea phase? Writer's block is the antithesis of creativity. Sure, there are days I must write when I'd much rather be doing something else. But I've got bills to pay. Writing is my career, and even if it's only a part-time endeavor for you, I'm guessing there is a financial reward that will keep your fingers at the keyboard.

Begin a writing session by polishing what you wrote yesterday. That can get creative energy flowing. Begin writing in the middle or end of your piece, a place where you feel more comfortable, or dictate notes into a tape recorder first. Truly visualize your article in the pages of the magazine you covet. If you must, take the book title you're working on and make up a dummy bestseller list, inserting your book's title. Look at this every day to remind you of where you want to be. Working to get there may not seem so daunting when you can clearly see the payoff. A handy little gem called *The Writer's Block: 786 Ideas to Jump-Start Your Imagination* by Jason Rekulak might do the trick if all else fails.

For ideas, keep pen and paper handy. Good ideas reveal themselves when you least expect it—at traffic lights, in grocery lines, and when you awaken at night. The change of scenery during vacations usually does it for me. Brainstorm what you know professionally, from hobbies, where you've been, and where you want to go. Do the same for everyone in your immediate circle. I'd be surprised if you still can't find a saleable topic. In addition, stay alert to what sells by scouring favorite publications.

Parents face other obstacles. It's a misconception that you'll never need child care when you work solo, but you can cut down on the expense. Take advantage of nap times, play dates, and preschool. Naysayers are obstacles. Socialize with supportive cheerleaders. Hang around winners. The camaraderie of other writers helps you to learn your craft. This book is also an important step toward that goal, and taking an organized class or attending a conference works wonders, too. It lends self-confidence and plain old chutzpah to move forward and fight timidity.

Path to More Profits

A committee appointed by the National Writers Union (NWU) Delegates Assembly found that rates have not always kept up with staff salaries, and that some magazines paid the same per-word rate in the late 1990s as they had thirty years prior. The median income of full-time college-educated workers in the United States was approximately $50,000. Thus, a freelance writer would need to command somewhere between $1.25 and $1.60 a word. Most magazines make their top pay rates $1 per word.

What is the use then, you might say. One of the most rewarding aspects to being a freelancer is control over your career, and that includes control over what types of assignments you seek.

For ongoing cash flow, invoice clients and follow through on contracts. If you're offered only a verbal commitment, nothing precludes you from drafting a memo of understanding. Add a line that says, "I hereby agree to the terms of this letter and agree to be legally bound by it." Provide a place for the recipient's signature and date, and ask that the letter be returned to you.

Never carry client expenses because this is a ticket into debt. Help clients establish accounts with printers, mailing houses, and other vendors and have all bills for these services be sent directly to the client. In the case of nonprofit organizations, this works to their advantage because of their tax-exempt status.

Target publishers who pay on acceptance rather than on publication. Who wants to wait months, possibly years for a paycheck? If you decide otherwise, focus on subjects you can produce easily or limit your sales to reprint rights. Don't factor this type of income into your budget. Consider it found money. If a pays-on-publication client lets its check writing slide, drop the client. I learned this when ninety days after publication, I was still waiting on a check because advertisers hadn't paid the publication yet. While I felt bad for this publisher, withholding payment showed a lack of regard for writers.

If you encounter a nonpaying client, send a strongly worded (but polite) letter or fax requesting payment; contact the accounting department; file a claim with a professional organization (the NWU can place a call for members with astonishing results); and/or take the matter to court. There will always be writers willing to accept low payment and put up with poor treatment. Look upon these clients as a way to produce needed clips as you start out. Then, move to higher income potential.

$$$-Making Prospects and Bargaining Power

Boost your bottom line by continually prospecting new sources of income. It can be financially risky to write for only one or two clients, and that is why this book can prove helpful to serious writers. It can lead you to new sources of income so that you aren't vulnerable to a recession in one industry.

Fast-cash prospects include fillers, greeting cards, brochures, client projects, and newspaper writing because dailies publish more frequently. Think seasonal such as back-to-school and holiday articles or when quarterly newsletters and annual reports are needed. Long-term income often stems from writing books, grant proposals, and PR campaigns; teaching; or commercial clients.

Stay visible, keep your marketing efforts alive, and approach dormant clients with proposals for new work. With every new assignment, be prepared to negotiate. Clients may have more latitude in terms of payment, but there is usually a set pay range at publications. Research a starting point, realizing that sometimes published rates are conservative numbers. I know some writers who honestly believe that if writers accept the first figure offered, they've undersold themselves.

List why you feel you deserve more than the typical rate, and be prepared to answer what makes you unique to this assignment. Factor into any discussions who pays for expenses, what rights you're selling (hint: maintain as many rights as possible), and a kill fee or amount paid if assignment is canceled. Remain client focused in what you bring to the bargaining table. Focus on the client's benefit and the value of your services, leaving out your business costs. Sure, you should factor these into your numbers, but only silently. If you've established a track record of consistently meeting client/editor needs, demand what you're worth. Sometimes it's wise to set rates and stick to them, particularly for commercial work. In fact, many writers I've interviewed refuse to bill anything less than $50 per hour, enlightening all concerned that they are not clerks and that their expertise has real value.

Be creative in negotiations. If you're writing for a trade association, ask for a free membership. If you could use additional books by the publisher, agree to be paid partly in credit toward material. Publishers have routinely done this by offering beginners a free magazine subscription in lieu of payment. I'm not advocating this beyond getting those first few clips, but every new project opens doors to obtain something you didn't have prior. Usually there is a middle ground so that you and your editor feel comfortable. Throw out figures about 10 to 15 percent higher than what you might ideally like in order not to undersell yourself.

If you are working on retainer, I'd encourage a written agreement establishing the maximum of hours worked, a price for overtime extended to your clients, and a review period that is mutually agreeable to both sides. This protects you from working at the same rate for years on end, and it relieves you of guessing when it would be appropriate to broach the subject of renegotiation. You'll feel more comfortable and be able to discuss money matters from a position of confidence and strength.

When pricing your services, it's wise to research what other writers charge in your area, and what the market will bear. You can do this by networking with informed sources, contacting writing organizations, and using books I've referenced in the Appendix. You could also estimate how much money you would like to earn per week. Divide that number by half the number of hours that you can reasonably work, and that will be your rate. The reason for using half the number of working hours available is that you must devote some time to marketing and administration. Or, assign greater value or a higher rate to some services over others.

Just be sure you're not overlooking items that most workers take for granted when they're accustomed to being an employee. This means you must add in 25 percent higher than what you might think for items such as benefits (vacation, medical, retirement, taxes, and overhead).

Some writers have been burned by quoting a project rate because invariably the job takes longer than either they or their client had anticipated. Formulate bids with the phrase "plus or minus 10 percent." If you finish under budget, everyone wins. To prevent low cash flow, writers also ask for some payment up front, much like book authors do when they receive the first installment of their advance against royalties. Another tactic is to seal your bids with a time frame such as "price good until . . ."

Keeping Careful Records

Keep a log of submissions, along with photocopies of cover letters, manuscripts, queries, and other correspondence, because this practice delineates your work as being business related and reminds you to follow up. A three-ring binder or filing system suits most writers. Use a similar method for recording income, invoices, expenses, car mileage, and computer usage. Record bank deposits with sufficient notation to explain the income if you're ever audited. Smaller publications frequently send checks without a perforated stub. Attach a photocopy to the invoice, and record the income in your ledger.

You don't need an accountant to keep good records. Create forms with a few columns and a series of lines. Record the mileage driven for business appointments, and if others use your computer, keep a computer log to track your time (for depreciation purposes). When vying for new business or negotiating higher fees, this notation pays off. If you've carefully logged your hours, you'll also have a head start compiling an accomplishment sheet. Also be sure to keep receipts of photocopies, subscriptions, software, membership, etc.

Copyright and Other Legal Concerns

Students invariably want to know, "Won't some editor rip off my work if I don't have a copyright?"

On any given day, editors must deal with the art and advertising departments, the publisher, meetings, and telephone calls, for starters. Some days they stay late and can't even find a bathroom break. While I understand such concern, trust me, the last motivation these editors wake up with is, "Gee, what writer will I rip off today?" Folks, it just doesn't happen on the level that beginners fear. I add that caveat because I cannot assure you that some unscrupulous editor in Podunk-town, U.S.A., won't steal your work. But I feel reasonably certain that you have better chances of winning the lottery. Why would an editor risk her job and thousands in legal fees for a magazine manuscript that costs (on average) a few hundred or less for her company to purchase?

If you've created a finished book or some extremely unique work—we're not talking query letters and magazine or newspaper features or card captions—then applying for a formal copyright protects you. But the project should warrant the trouble and expense. If you call (202) 707-3000 or log on to www.copyright.gov/register, you'll find a wealth of information on registering copyrights. To register a book, for instance, you should send the appropriate filled-out form (Copyright Form TX), a check for the $30 registration fee, and nonreturnable copies of the to-be-registered work to the Library of Congress.

Under the Copyright Act (Title 17 of the U.S. code), as of March 1, 1989, copyright exists by mere fact that someone created the work, and not by whether notice has been posted. Notices are no longer mandatory as they were prior to March 1989. For work sent to most publishers, you risk branding yourself the amateur if you display the copyright symbol unnecessarily. However, if you circulate material widely (as I do with teaching handouts) then displaying the proper notice does prevent possible infringement. Use your best judgment. The correct notice reads "Copyright [dates] by [author/owner]" or with the "C" in a circle (the official copyright symbol) (for example, © 2004 by Loriann Hoff Oberlin). While registration is not required for copyright to exist, it's necessary to a successful infringement suit. Most claims, though, are settled out of court.

If you want to cite copyrighted material in your own work, you should seek a formal permission from the copyright holder. If you're merely excerpting a fraction of the work, you may not even need to seek a formal permission provided you quote accurately and note any sources. But you must judge the ratio of work to excerpt. The doctrine of "fair use" allows for copyrighted material to be cited for research, teaching, news reporting, criticism, limited publicity, and similar purposes. We've seen startling headlines in recent years in which prolific authors have literally tripped over their own footnotes. Two cases occurred

with bestselling historians and another with a famed women's fiction author. What literary faux pas did these writers make? They either sloppily
or unknowingly lifted entire passages of other people's work, claiming it
as their own in books they churned out like an assembly line. Some did
not use quotation marks to cite passages belonging to another author.
This activity is called *plagiarism,* and it's not a kind word. Essentially,
plagiarism is stealing another writer's work, including a replication of
vivid detail and sequence of thought. Citing another author's words can
be done legally and ethically if you follow the prescribed procedures of
seeking permission, quoting, and citing your sources. Many authors are
grateful for the publicity. In another example of irresponsible writing,
one case made headlines where it was discovered that a reporter at a
prestigious newspaper was not merely sloppy in his reporting but had
completely fabricated interviews and quoted passages. Those who yearn
to invent fiction should concentrate on novels.

For books, most standard contracts call for the publisher to apply
for the copyright in the author's name. Double-checking the copyright on a book is a good indication of a royalty-based book or
whether it's a work-for-hire project. If the publisher owns the copyright, it may be a work for hire.

Any serious journalist should have a working knowledge of libel,
which refers to printed or broadcast communication where a statement injures reputation by holding someone else up to hatred or
ridicule, contempt, ostracism, or extreme mental anguish and humili-
ation. Of course, truth is the best defense against libel, but the onus
may fall upon the writer to prove it. That is why when wannabe novelists ask if they can portray a character based upon someone in real
life, they are best served if they combine traits from many sources to
create an entirely unique character. The supposed victim must also
prove actual economic damage or mental anguish. It is also significant
whether the alleged assault took place against a private or public person. People who have thrust themselves into the public arena must
prove malice or that the journalist made the statement with a reckless
disregard for the truth. It is somewhat different for private persons,
but the bottom line here remains—get your facts entirely straight. In
nonfiction, writers also are better served with composites of various
people, and a disclaimer stating this up front. Health writers, especially, follow this policy so as not to identify a patient.

Tax Advantages

Because tax laws change each year, I suggest you go straight to the regulations or the tax professionals for the best information. Come tax time, you can also use computer software tax preparation packages. But since there are tax advantages to self-employment, I'll offer suggestions so that you collect the receipts and records you need all year long. Worst case: Your writing looks more like a hobby than a business, in which case you toss the paperwork, but you'll know what you need to collect.

To take advantage of tax deductions, your writing must clearly be recognized as a business rather than a hobby. The IRS requires that you earn a profit in three of the past five years. You must carry on your writing in a businesslike, profitable manner, and you must possess the knowledge required—that is, you can't be an anesthesiologist with a bachelor's degree.

In order to take the home office deduction, your home office must be used solely for business purposes. That regulation may disqualify a spare bedroom, den, or corner of a kitchen. I know some self-employed people who frown upon taking the deduction because they fear it will raise red flags. Others say if you're entitled to it, take it—as long as you have the data to back it up.

Every trip to the library, every trip to photocopy your clips, and every trip to interview someone are all legitimate business errands to track in a mileage log with the date of trip; purpose; and starting, ending, and total mileage. Deduct office supplies and equipment noted in this chapter. Equipment can be depreciated over several years, and if others use the computer, keep a log of your use. It can also be written off in one installment, but check your regulations. Personal finance magazines, newspaper articles, tax guides, and books about self-employment will guide you, and, if necessary, consult a tax adviser. The money-management program Quicken imports data directly into TurboTax, thereby aiding record keeping.

Bounce Back from Rejection

Accept rejection as an ordinary occurrence of the writing life. Anticipate it. Dare I say, even embrace it. Sometimes rejection occurs for
good reason. I've found you can learn something from most every rejection, and that by slight revision or better honing of the topic, you're
on sturdier ground.

Editors reject manuscripts and queries for many reasons. Perhaps
your idea was already assigned to another writer or was staff written.
Maybe it's slated to appear in the next issue. Perhaps your query wasn't
targeted enough. Most publishers must meet their advertisers' needs,
because advertising often pays for magazines. If your idea doesn't support existing or future advertising, it could be golden, but it's not likely
to be published.

Limited rejections won't stifle your career. While a few have stung
me, I've persevered and reminded myself of my successes. I urge you
to give yourself the same pep talk. Move on. Reroute rejected material
to other markets, or you'll never know what sale awaits you.

Ward off writing blues with regular breaks, especially for exercise.
You'll do your body, mind, and creativity a favor. Change your at-
mosphere. Take your laptop to the library. Do research at your favorite bookstore. I don't know about you, but I feel at home in most
bookstores, and if there's a coffee shop with the simmering scent of
freshly baked scones . . . well, this eases rejection also, although too
much caffeine may plummet your productivity later. Another pick-
me-up: Position your work space near natural light. Keep in touch
with colleagues and friends if the work becomes too solitary. Writing
is intensely introspective, so you need to ward against taking rejection and isolation too personally.

CHAPTER 3

Developing Journalistic Style

IT DOESN'T MATTER WHICH FREELANCE AREA YOU CHOOSE, EACH ONE requires clear and concise writing; good grammar, vocabulary usage, and spelling; and a smooth journalistic style. If you think your current education yields a deficit, you still don't need even one journalism course. What I offer here will equip you with a basic knowledge of journalism, which is your ticket to landing assignments and earning income.

Routinely, I've taken a wide body of information and presented it in neatly wrapped packages, such as ten-second public service announcements (PSAs) during an internship at a television station, advertising catalog copy for a retailer, and newsletter text for many clients. Every word *must* work. With practice this becomes inherent, and with each article you edit, you'll trim unnecessary verbiage to write tight.

The Five "W"s and the "H"

These are the foundations of all journalistic writing: who, what, when, where, why, and how. These essential questions give your reader (or listener) a clear grasp of information. Leave one out, and you'll cause a certain amount of chaos.

Imagine the listener tuning into his radio. Music creates ambiance while you cook dinner, wash the car, or sit down at work. The disc jockey reads a PSA for a benefit concert this weekend, only the spot never mentions when it will begin. The listener might just show up at the time these events normally occur. What if he is wrong and shows up an hour after the performance has begun? His wife yells at him for not getting the information straight. They've both just blown a Saturday evening, wasted money on a baby-sitter, and now they're angry with one another.

Okay, so my example might be a little far-fetched. The point is that much information, whether it is written or broadcast, competes for our time. Forget an essential fact, and the communication fails on two counts. Your job as a writer is to make life easier on people, not harder. So remember the five "W"s and the "H."

In my writing classes, I often add a sixth "W." I ask, "Who cares?" Though I usually get a chuckle, I'm not being flippant. No matter what form of writing in which you concentrate—fillers and greeting cards, feature articles, scholarly journals, book writing, or business and technical assignments—there must be an audience that cares. If not, your carefully crafted words aren't going to sell. That's our purpose after all—to generate income. If few people care, rework your topic.

Interviews—The Search for Answers

Now that you recognize the importance of the five "W"s and the "H," how do you get the answers to them? Enter the interview, the technique writers use to extract information from valuable sources.

Interviews bring real, live people and substance to our writing. Since many writers are generalists, relying upon a broad base of knowledge, we require other insights, perceptions, reactions, and feelings to guide us through each topic's unfamiliar territory. Other times, the people we interview can relate experience and offer explanations far better than we can. Good writing thrives on diversity. Readers enjoy other people's opinions. Sure, we could summarize their facts for them, but just as witnesses add drama with their own words in a courtroom, so do most people's words when they create word pictures for us.

Interviewing becomes an essential skill, whether it is in person, by telephone, or through some mail/e-mail/fax combination. Nothing can replace the ease of e-mail, which can eliminate the unnecessary telephone tag that invariably transpires with busy schedules. When a personal visit is impractical, interviewing like this offers convenience, saving time and money. If you're only being paid seventy-five dollars to write a story, traveling across town or even for twenty minutes eats into your income with expense. Unless you're doing in-depth profiles, question-and-answer pieces, or extensive research, a telephone interview or e-mailing questions should suffice.

Finding the Right Authority

If you read widely, you'll remain attuned to experts, both local and national, who might have something to offer your projects. We interview and quote people because they have the business acumen, professional experiences, or life story to make our readers' eyes widen. Develop a keen ear to what reporters are saying on a newscast or talk show, because this might help you to find experts. Keep some blank tapes nearby in case you want to record a program in its entirety.

Internet searches make finding authorities much more manageable than when I began freelancing in the 1980s. In fact, if you missed watching a leading expert being interviewed on *20/20* last night, you can use search engines, network Web sites, and electronic library services to retrieve the text of many interviews you may need. Develop the habit of carrying paper and a pen with you at all times. When you spot appropriate information or a beneficial source, you'll be prepared to write it down.

Research Made Simple

Draw up a list of questions before any telephone or personal interview. Get as much information as possible. The Internet makes research a snap or, at the very least, awfully convenient on a snowy day.

If ordinary search engines don't uncover needed material, subscribe to an online electronic library service that has access to thousands of newspapers, magazines, books, tapes, and interviews. Some libraries still offer the *Reader's Guide to Periodical Literature*. More often, librarians use software, search engines, or an electronic journal service such as EBSCOhost. Make friends of your librarians. Their knowledge and ease of finding material are resources that can advance your career. Besides, they love the written word, just like you do. Even from a distance, you can access their research prowess. Many county libraries have a reference desk where a librarian can look up brief items.

Public relations sites are available for journalists to post questions, which are then forwarded to literally thousands or millions of PR professionals. Be careful not to divulge your telephone number, unless you want to be inundated. Check out the Appendix for additional resources.

If your library doesn't stock the publication you need, you can request it through interlibrary loan. If your subject is local, ask community leaders, the person's secretary, or the person himself for background material. Most people will be more than willing to oblige.

For in-depth assignments, do a thorough background search, remembering that more is preferable to less. Proper research saves time. Time is money. Don't spend the precious moments with your interviewee seeking answers to questions you could have obtained elsewhere. People are on tight schedules. State which magazine assigned you or whether you're using the interview for a spec submission, because most people want to know the publication in which they'll appear. Always request permission before using their quotes in another story, or discuss the possibility ahead of time.

Completing Your Interview

After some get-acquainted conversation, get down to business. Ask whether it is all right to use a tape recorder. Because technology has been known to fail, always take notes to obtain accurate quotations.

Early on, take charge and begin your questions. It's easy to become carried away in conversation; however, remember why you're there. Get to the heart of the subject, but save the probing questions for the middle of the interview. By this time you will have developed a certain rapport, and you'll solicit better responses. If you wait until the very end, your time may be cut short.

Unless you want yes or no answers, ask open-ended, attitudinal questions beginning with "how" or "why." These types of questions probe deeper. If your subject stops short, ask him or her to expand upon the last answer or cite specific examples. When you must cover controversial or sensitive subject matter, lead in by saying, "Critics charge . . ." or "It's been said . . ." Watch the pros on television to see how they navigate difficult questions. It's wise to rephrase questions when you're tempted to start with "you" or "your," because these words come off as critical.

Always recheck the accuracy of spellings and quotations. Because memories fade, transcribe any tapes and fill in your notes as soon as possible. Finally, remember that editors often demand fact-checking data to confirm what sources told you. There is no fudging here, or you fail freelancing big time. Beware of unconfirmed material, biased sources, press releases, and even previously published material. There could still be mistakes or severe slanting. Keep digging even after the interview to confirm items you discovered.

Inside the Quotation Marks

We quote other people because quotes lend authority to our work, and the mere presence of quotation marks tells readers to sit up and take notice because someone else is about to take stage. Very simply, quotations have undeniable power. They're emblazoned on T-shirts, embroidered onto pillows, and plastered onto bumper stickers. Just the right quote can give us personal insight, new information, or a summary of the argument or point we're trying to make.

But if you choose the wrong material to encase in quotations, you and your subject can look foolish. For instance, quotation marks do not make clichés legitimate. More on clichés in a moment, but remember that whatever you put inside those marks immediately cues importance. If you waste that precious moment on something poor, you've brought attention all right, but for all the wrong reasons.

Decide what you'll paraphrase and save the best statements for quotations. Don't quote a nurse saying, "I'm going to take your blood pressure now." Most nurses say that. A quotation like that one tells the reader nothing new. Only commit quotation marks around something that would raise an eyebrow or force interest. "Oh my, I'd better get the doctor" would leave the reader wanting to know more.

When quoting, always try to put your subject in the best possible light. Unless including an error in language serves a purpose—for example, when quoting young children or the uneducated—I'd mend any minor mistakes in grammar or syntax. We're all a little more casual about our speech than writing.

Don't relinquish control of your article to your interviewees either. A carefully chosen and well-placed quote, here and there, complements your own style. Too much and it weakens your writing. This occurs, in particular, with extremely long passages of quotes. If you're faced with so many sentences, at the very least, attribute these thoughts to someone midway through your writing. Don't let the reader wait until six sentences to find out who owns the words or theories.

Instead of trying out every synonym for "said" or "says," just use the words, okay? I say this because writers rack their minds for all possibilities, feeling guilty if they count too many uses of "said" or "says." They'll have people exclaiming; shouting; and what's far worse, using verbs that aren't even affiliated with a speaking action. It's completely unnecessary. It's another way that writers call attention to their writing for foolish reasons. The human eye and ear are tuned to overlook "said" or "says."

One last thing: Occasionally your interviewee will ask if he can look at your article before you submit it. Previewing equals censorship. Reporters work uncensored, free of such constraints. Given the chance, sources might change their recollections or words to a more acceptable point of view. Also, by giving this kind of advantage to one source, you give that person unfair insight into information from other sources. Clearly identify yourself as a journalist researching a story for publication. Take great care in quoting people and review any spellings, titles, or troublesome quotes for accuracy. *You* read these to *them,* not the other way around.

Eliminating Clichés

Clichés surround us. We become so accustomed to phrases such as "don't want to rock the boat," "pick up the tab," "in my book," or "better late than never" that we don't always recognize them or even agree that our chosen words are indeed clichéd.

Each profession has its own pat phrases. We call this jargon. The problem is that both clichés and jargon weaken our writing by opting for the lazy, unimaginative way out and by trying to impress.

Instead of using a cliché to hedge or quickly commit words to your screen, use words that are fresh, inspiring new thoughts, not old standbys. With jargon, resist the temptation unless you are very certain your audience is made up strictly of peers. For example, if a speech therapist treating your child asks, "Are the dysfluencies still present?" she really means, "Does your child still stutter?" The word "stutter," while to the point, might be struck from a professional's vocabulary as stigmatizing, but the situation probably calls for the most easily understood word. However, the word "dysfluencies" just doesn't cut it with a parent, in my opinion. As a rule to write by (note I could have said "rule of thumb" but caught myself!), any time you can say something in five letters rather than fifteen, go for the easier, more direct route. Use a fresh phrase, not a stale one.

Lastly, patrol your prose for empty words or phrases we tack on needlessly to our sentences—such as "very," "hopefully," "extremely," or "for all intents and purposes." Strike these and you'll be a much more effective writer.

Writing in the Inverted Pyramid

If you ever took a journalism class, you might remember that classic drawing of the upside-down triangle, otherwise known as the inverted pyramid. Instructors test geometric skills to demonstrate an important writing concept. The drawing depicts the fullness that is embodied at the top of whatever you write. All important information belongs in the beginning of your story.

I'm referring to the material we covered earlier—the who, what, when, where, why, and how. These questions deserve answers in your lead sentence, where your reader will develop an interest in your story or pass it over. A lead sentence or paragraph creates a mood. It says to your reader, "You're going to smile while you read this story," "Get the box of tissues ready," or "When you put this down, you'll be compelled to act." Whatever the result, your lead grabs your reader and sets the foundation for what follows.

The inverted pyramid is used more often in newspaper writing than in magazine formats. Why? Because newspaper editors must fit your copy into prescribed column inches that could be drastically reduced on a heavy news day. If a terrorist attack or stock market decline becomes the top story, your words, no matter how carefully crafted, may need to be reduced. Editors do that from the bottom up at a newspaper, whereas at a magazine, features fill prescribed pages, not inches. Usually, if a magazine is reduced in size (because of low advertising sales or breaking news), a story is generally held, not shortened.

Action Counts

Pretend you're reading your favorite newspaper. Now compare these two sentences:

> The bill was passed last night by members of both the House of Representatives and the U.S. Senate, including ranking Democrats who argued favorably for change.

Okay, that sentence tells you something, but I'm going to argue for another take:

> Convinced by Democratic petitions for change, the House and Senate passed the bill in a late-night session.

I'd argue that the second sentence is much more powerful. Why? Right off, it's shorter, easier on the eyes (or ears). It gets to the point. The first sentence contains superfluous detail. The most telling reason is that the second sentence provides action and takes more responsibility.

Does your writing skip or simply stroll along? Do your words evoke images so that readers can see and believe instead of read and merely trust? Action is power. A carefully chosen action verb incites readers to visualize, think, and even question what is written. That is what good writing is all about, folks.

Writing with action sells manuscripts. It's called the active voice. It's crisp. It's clear. It communicates using far fewer words. Ever wonder why so many academic, bureaucratic, and legal documents get plagued by the passive voice? No surprise there! It's easy, less risky. No one has to put a name on it. No one has to take responsibility. Changing your sentences from the passive to the active voice might not make every sentence dance, but it will pack a lot more punch into what you say.

One way to spot the passive voice is to recognize forms of the verb "be" such as "is," "are," "was," "were," and "been." With practice, you'll develop the first-aid measure of eliminating passive construction, rewriting so that the subject acts. Trust me, experience makes this easier.

In the classic writing book *The Elements of Style,* the late Professor William Strunk, Jr., wrote, "Vigorous writing is concise. A sentence should contain no unnecessary words, a paragraph no unnecessary sentences, for the same reason that a drawing should have no unnecessary lines and a machine no unnecessary parts."[1]

When you sit down with your first draft, always ask: Does every word work? In many cases, you'll find words that deserve to be pruned. While *The Elements of Style* doesn't quite rank up there with a Grisham novel, review it periodically. It's a handy tool.

Exceptions to Every Rule

Abraham Lincoln probably didn't use such wisdom when uttering the Gettysburg Address. What about the Bible? Famous literary passages? If we rewrite passive constructions in these famous works, don't we ruin the beauty of the language?

Yes, on all counts. Take the Bible passage that is read at many Christian weddings—I Corinthians 13:2–3. In the Revised Standard Version of the Bible, it reads:

> If I speak in the tongues of men and of angels, but have not love, I am a noisy gong or a clanging cymbal. And if I have prophetic powers, and understand all mysteries and all knowledge, and if I have all faith, so as to remove mountains, but have not love, I am nothing.

Then, look at *The Living Bible* version:

> If I had the gift of being able to speak in other languages without learning them, and could speak in every language there is in all of heaven and earth, but didn't love others, I would only be making noise. If I had the gift of prophecy and knew all about what is going to happen in the future, knew everything about *everything,* but didn't love others, what

good would it do? Even if I had the gift of faith so that I could
speak to a mountain and make it move, I would still be worth
nothing at all without love.

Which passage is richer? Which calls out more to a person? Which
is more concise? Admittedly, *The Living Bible* is a paraphrased version. To me, though, there is no comparison between the two, and as
a writer, I would choose to maintain the integrity of the older version
rather than sacrifice the beauty for newer, trendier words.

It's also important to remember that while we must edit language
for clarity, we shouldn't sacrifice colorful language. In some instances,
colloquial flavor; regional dialect; historical context; and yes, even a
swear word, might be called for.

While discussing rules, how about reading that last sentence one
more time. I ended with a preposition, didn't I? But your grammar
teacher told you not to, right? There I go again, starting a sentence
with "and" or "but." Who is correct?

As in all things, times change and so do the dictates that guide us.
Nearly fifteen years ago, Diana Hacker, known by some as the Queen
of the Comma, wrote *A Writer's Reference*. It soon became the fastest-
selling textbook in the United States. Hacker gives her blessing to beginning a sentence with "and" or "but," despite diehard grammarians.

Never end a sentence with a preposition? That too is more acceptable these days. In *The Creative Writer's Style Guide*, Christopher T. Leland claims exceptions to the hard-and-fast rule. You
wouldn't write, "Don't screw up it," he says, so stick with "Don't
screw it up." If you can avoid ending with a preposition, do so. If
not, just don't make your sentence absurd. Leland tells readers that
this dilemma stemmed from misguided souls attempting to impose
the rules of Latin grammar on the English language centuries ago.
Sir Winston Churchill gave a most ludicrous example of this taken to
the extreme with "This is the sort of English up with which I will not
put." Get the idea?

Style is a very important matter. Let your goals guide your purchase
of Associated Press style (for news), American Psychological Association (APA) style (for researchers, psychologists, or other behavioral
sciences), or *The Chicago Manual of Style* (for scholars, editors, and
publishers).

The Importance of Your Lead

It doesn't matter how fascinating the middle of your story is, or how compellingly you close your piece, if your lead doesn't grab your readers, they—or worse yet, your editor—will put it aside.

The lead is that first sentence(s) that tells readers what is in it for them. It creates a mood, grabs attention, and promises to deliver new information, something useful and full of value, excitement, controversy, and maybe even fun. The failure to deliver is fatal because your lead creates impressions.

It's easy to start a lead with a quotation, but that is not advisable. My goal here is to stretch your imagination. From the first word, establish that you, not your subject, are in control of the piece. Introduce your topic, and then let another person speak. It's much more effective this way. In addition, I would caution the beginning writer against starting with a question, because you don't want to rely on this easy technique that may thwart a more creative lead.

As leads go, I always tell my students to recognize two types: the direct and the delayed. The direct lead is often used in hard news—front-page reporting where you need the facts, and fast. Sometimes, this is called a nut graph or billboard paragraph. In features or slightly "softer" news, writers can employ the delayed lead where they can toy with the reader, by taking time to get to the point. In a sense, it's license to have fun with the topic. Even if you use a delayed lead, a nut graph usually follows that conveys the exact scope of your article. Read the sidebar called "Successful Article Openings" for examples of winning leads or consult *Leads & Conclusions* by Marshall J. Cook.

Concluding Your Story

In a conclusion, quotations can work well to summarize your exact point (as opposed to quotes in leads). It's okay here to let someone else have the final say. Many quotes have long-lasting impact. So do anecdotes that describe a firsthand situation as well as a basic restatement of your theme. Your ending needs to wind down your story and have a sense of closure. Just as a good novel has that perfect feel when you end it, trust your instinct. If you want readers to ponder, frame

Successful Article Openings

There are two primary types of leads: direct for hard news and delayed for feature writing. It's quite possible to have a combination of the two types. Here are three good examples:

From the front page of the *Washington Post,* September 12, 2001:

> Terrorists unleashed an astonishing air assault on America's military and financial power centers yesterday morning, hijacking four commercial jets and then crashing them into the World Trade Center in New York, the Pentagon, and the Pennsylvania countryside.*

Analysis: No one wants to have delayed news for something like a terrorist attack. This direct lead tells readers in one concrete sentence what happened and where, and, just like war, when loved ones might be deployed overseas. Imagine the readers' frustration and anger if the reporter had taken his time getting to the point. Hard news is no place to play around. Give it straight. Give it accurately. Then move on to other details readers need to know.

From the *Pittsburgh Post-Gazette,* October 12, 1998:

> A Pittsburgh mom and her 21-year-old daughter are being lured to Detroit on the promise of a bigger house, a bigger pool, and quite possibly, sexual favors.
>
> The sluts. Maybe you've seen 'em. The mother is a 30-year-old polar bear at the Pittsburgh Zoo and the daughter is the big white carnivore with whom she shares the popular exhibit, where they swim in their pool and pace the rocky ledge behind it.†

---

*Michael Grunwald, "Terrorists Hijack 4 Airliners, Destroy World Trade Center, Hit Pentagon," *The Washington Post,* September 12, 2001. © 2001, *The Washington Post.*
†Gene Collier, "It's Unbearable: Zoo's Pair Trades Pittsburgh Pad for Cooler Digs," *Pittsburgh Post-Gazette,* October 12, 1998. © 1998, *Pittsburgh Post-Gazette.* All rights reserved. Reprinted with permission.

Analysis: This is one of my all-time favorites. It's a classic example of leading the reader in one direction, then surprising with new information and a laugh. Most certainly this is a delayed lead, and that makes sense for this soft news feature story. Lifestyle and feature writers use this technique to pace their article as a tale, often tempting the reader with a morsel at a time.

From the *Arizona Republic,* May 17, 2002:

It's easier to track a UPS package than a student in Arizona. The Department of Education released its annual dropout study Thursday, saying the number of kids quitting Arizona's high schools declined to 9.8 percent during the 2000–2001 school year, down from 11.1 percent the year before.*

Analysis: This is what I'd term a combination approach. No doubt the topic is serious, yet it's not life or death. The first sentence whets your interest to read further. Next, it moves to summarizing the facts.

your conclusion that way. Many times, you'll want to give readers room to reflect on what they just read. End with the best material you can muster.

Educational Requirements for Writers

Writing like a journalist is not rocket science. While I don't want to diminish anyone who has spent four years majoring in the subject, I don't believe you need the degree to write well. I once lamented that during high school, I felt cheated because I couldn't take journalism, which met the same period as band, until my senior year, when the schedule shifted. "We can see how that really held you back," some-

---

*Pat Kossan, "Dropout Data for Arizona 'A Mess'," *Arizona Republic,* May 17, 2002. © 2002, *Arizona Republic.* Used with permission. Permission does not imply endorsement.

one teased. I've authored hundreds of articles and countless collateral material. This is my seventh book, and I'm sure there will be other outlets for my work.

Having said that, I often hear the same lament. One student in my writing class wished she had majored in journalism instead of nursing. I asked her, "Are you kidding? Do you know how many articles you'll get a shot at authoring with R.N. credentials?" Often another degree or credential will help establish you far faster as an authority, opening more editorial doors, as long as you can write well.

Degree status truly depends on your goals. Credentials matter in health care and professional fields. A computer science degree coupled with writing prowess is a ticket to technical writing. For the aspiring writer who sees himself or herself as a generalist, liberal arts education is crucial. I've used my liberal arts background every single day because I've had to interview and write about health, law, business, psychology and relationships, parenting, technical matters, entertainment, the arts, and more. There may come a point, however, where you delineate a more narrow range of topics that interest you, or where you have the opportunity to publish. For example, an RN will have a leg up on health assignments and a degree in counseling might open doors to advice columns and similar assignments. If an advanced degree makes sense, go for it.

If you want to teach writing in higher education, some suggest that a Master of Fine Arts (M.F.A.) is the terminal degree. Others would argue for a Ph.D. in English. When I was contemplating graduate degrees, one of my college professors told me not to bother with an M.F.A., because my publishing credits already put me beyond that level. I've also been told that the competition among students in M.F.A. programs can be brutal. While the goal is to learn from peers, if 150 students vie for one or two program scholarships, the careful criticism hoped for in class can turn into tension. Also, the cost (and debt) of a graduate degree must be weighed against the potential payback. A law or medical degree almost guarantees future higher income. Writers aren't as fortunate. Carefully weigh your educational options with your career progression and goals. Consider more education to expand your employment prospects if you believe you can truly leverage the added knowledge or credentials conferred into obtaining more writing assignments, higher fees, or book advances.

Brushing Up on Grammar and Vocabulary

A good working knowledge of English grammar goes a long way for anyone—writer or not. What if you forgot all those lessons of long ago? Don't despair. Today there are many books to help you brush up on remedial grammar and spelling. The Appendix lists several.

Grammar and spelling are intrinsic to the way we think, with elements that are unique to every culture and language. Grammar is the foundation of everything the writer creates. In this age of having spelling and grammar checks as features of popular word-processing software, it's tempting to let the computer do all the work. However, writers must have a strong command of the language, which also improves their chances of landing freelance copyediting or proofreading jobs. So invest in one of these books, and check out the resources of www.grammarlady.com and www.grammarqueen.com.

As for broadening your vocabulary, nothing expands it more than avid reading. I suggest that you choose words and phrases with care. Avoid euphemisms just as you would clichés. Be specific. For instance, we don't "lose" workers, we "fire," "lay off," or "transfer" workers.

Careful Choices for the Times

Just as clichés are built into our vocabulary, so is sexist language. In fact, in a multicultural society, it's best to carefully scrutinize your writing. If you offend any group with offensive words, it signals a lack of professionalism and puts your editor on guard for future slipups.

Find alternatives to words such as "businessman," "fireman," "salesman," "stewardess," and "watchman." Let's call a receptionist just that, not the "girl in the office." I know women who aren't bothered by that, but think about the nuances. The word "girl" connotes something entirely different from "woman" or even "lady." You have a harder time envisioning a girl or lady running a company or campaigning for Congress, don't you?

Replacing hackneyed expressions with more socially conscious choices is challenging. It's easier to switch between using "he" and

Manuscript Mechanics

If I had used proper manuscript form when I began freelancing, I would have saved myself a major mishap. Turns out a manuscript I'd mailed on spec made it to print, only I was never informed. My cover letter was separated from the article, and without my name, address, and telephone number placed in the upper left-hand corner, no one knew where to find me or where to send payment.

Directly across from these items, to the right, you should indicate what rights you are selling, and underneath, an estimate of the manuscript's length. Just indicate "About 1,000 words." I usually reserve that third line for my e-mail address. You can use the copyright symbol, but I already expressed reservations about that. Each case is different. Don't brand yourself a beginner with its overuse.

Skip a few spaces and center your title with your byline underneath. Drop another two or three lines and begin your manuscript, remembering to type double space. On all subsequent pages, type one or two words as the header identifying the manuscript and your last name, separated by a slash mark. Then, put the page number. When you come to the end of your story, indicate the conclusion by typing "—30—" or "—###—," which are standard symbols recognized throughout the writing industry.

When formatting a manuscript, leave ample room in the margins for an editor's notations. This usually means one-inch margins on all sides. Do this, even if you think the material will be edited in electronic form. I place a vertical staple in the upper left corner, but only for short articles. Never try to staple long manuscripts. These should be secured with a rubber band. Today, many editors are happy to receive an e-mail file attachment, eliminating your weighing manuscripts at the post office. I'd still advise printing out your manuscript to spot more errors on paper versus scrolling down a computer screen, and I'd ask first before sending any attached files to editors, who may be fearful of downloads and computer viruses.

Whenever you make a submission to a new editor, always enclose a self-addressed, stamped envelope (known industry-wide as the SASE). If you need to know how to prepare and present other types of projects, consult *The Writer's Digest Guide to Manuscript Formats* by Dian Dincin Buchman and Seli Groves.

"she," but many writers (and readers) find this technique to be distracting, not to mention wordy. Other alternatives: Rewrite your sentences in the plural, replacing "he" with the second-person "you," or substitute the first-person plural "we/us/our" instead of "he/him/his. For example, "Writers must avoid sexist language whenever they can" instead of "a writer must avoid sexist language whenever he or she can."

Painting Word Pictures

Advertisers have long understood the emotional connection between carefully chosen words and the ability to inspire people to action. That's why we writers can take a lesson from them in painting word pictures—vivid images of what we mean so that the reader can actually see what we're discussing. It's an approach that relationship experts use as well. For instance, if a wife is trying to convey feelings to her husband, she is wise to think of what he understands most. If it's his car, she might use the analogy "When we don't eat together as a family, it's like you skipping regular maintenance on your car. It just won't run as well." Whereas he might have dismissed her concerns about dinner, perhaps now he can better understand the significance. Descriptive examples and sharing stories or anecdotes can paint word pictures. So does format. You might use bullets and parallel construction to get your reader to picture what you're expressing. One brochure describes, "Our lakeside lodge caters to every need of diverse groups." But it's not as compelling as, "Our lakeside lodge offers a wing of conference rooms so that your group stays together; two-bedroom suites for traveling families seeking privacy; and kitchenettes with complimentary coffee so that you can enjoy your first cup on your private balcony or patio."

This type of description helps the reader put himself or herself into the situation. Marketing pros could tell you that a person is much more likely to book a reservation after reading the second description. You don't need to be selling a product to employ this technique. Some experts believe that people who are more right-brain dominant are more feelings oriented, preferring anecdotes and endorsements. If you design a page layout with this in mind, remember that readers process bullets and lists much better. The left-brain-oriented crowd tends to be logical, relying on facts and figures. Why does the writer care? Because lists are easy, and they make editors (and readers) take notice. Balance the presentation of your material so that all readers walk away having learned something.

Good Writing = Revision

Few people realize the amount of revision that goes into the craft of writing. It's rarely correct the first time, and if you expect your prose to be perfect after putting aside the pen, you're setting yourself up for a fall. Instead, learn to revise your work. Pay close attention to the technical side of writing (grammar, spelling, and punctuation) as well as content (fact checking and style). Also, answer the following questions to ensure that your finished piece is ready to send off to your editor:

- Does my lead grab readers' attention, forcing them to remain with me? Have I included important elements my readers need to know up front?

- Is my message clear, concise, and correct? Is it conversational when appropriate?

- Do I hide behind the passive voice? Or, do my verbs shout action?

- Do my sentences limp along or lunge forward, propelling readers to a new level of understanding?

✐ Are my sentences diverse enough? Of varying lengths? Or, do they cry out in sing-song "subject, verb . . . subject, verb" format?

✐ Have I weeded out all empty or unnecessary words or phrases? Clichés? Offensive language?

✐ Have I painted word pictures so that my readers can "see" what I'm writing about? Do my words evoke images?

✐ Do my quotations or dialogue sound natural when read aloud or stilted? Have I used quotation marks to identify ideas that any fool could have said, or have I used them when I truly felt the information would cause a few heads to turn?

✐ Have I created good transitions between paragraphs? Have I used sidebars for ancillary material?

✐ If I had to write especially tight, did I use well-organized bullets or lists for the main points, thus eliminating transitions?

✐ Does my conclusion wind down the story and have a sense of closure about it?

✐ Is my manuscript formatted according to professional standards?

Recommended Software for Writers

A writer cannot work effectively without the proper tools and software. In researching this book, I looked at dozens of products. While I'll mention a few more in later sections, here are my seven recommendations for general products writers should consider purchasing:

1. **Microsoft Office.** Granted, Office XP Professional comes with Access (not on the Mac platform), but overall this is a gem because of Microsoft Word, which has become standard in many editorial offices. If you can master the other programs such as PowerPoint (frequently used in teaching and speaking for visual effect) as well as Excel (for data), you're even further ahead.

2. **Adobe Acrobat Reader.** While many writers have the free download to read portable document format (PDF) files, the full software package lets you create a work with layout, fonts, links, and images that remain intact when opened. This is especially necessary for producing e-books. The software allows you to convert other documents or Web pages into PDF files, create interactive forms with pop-up boxes, buttons and text fields, and a lot more. It's made for both PC and Mac platforms.

3. **Norton Internet Security.** With Internet use and the exchange of e-mail and attached files comes great risk. But we writers can't commit ourselves to the closet, so the next best thing is proper protection for our computer systems. Symantec Corporation developed this all-inclusive product with its well-known antivirus, personal firewall, and privacy control components. Your files and e-mail (on either a PC or Mac) will be automatically scanned for viruses that can disable your computer and infect other people's computers (worst case, your editor's!). What's more, you'll safeguard confidential information and keep hackers at bay.

4. **Mavis Beacon Teaches Typing.** By far, the high school class I still reap benefits from is typing. Called keyboarding today, the lack of this skill seriously impairs any writer. This program speeds your work if you merely peck at the keyboard. Broderbund made this product bilingual for Spanish-speaking users. There is a Mac version available.

5. **Encarta Reference Library 2003.** Microsoft updates its CD-ROM encyclopedia each year, so this is a handy tool if your work entails much fact checking. It will be a tremendous help in locating and using statistics, footnoted material, charts and tables, an interactive world atlas, relevant Web and video links, quotations, as well as dictionary and thesaurus entries. It's like having an entire library reference room in your home office. Only on PC, but online accessible by Mac and PC.

6. **Broderbund Print Shop.** This product is available on both PC and Mac (though the deluxe version is PC only) and includes thousands of stock photography and graphic art images and templates for use in designing professional stationery, newsletters, promotional pieces, and other documents. It even allows you to edit photos, video, and music. If you produce graphics and text routinely, your best bet may be page layout software such as Pagemaker and a more versatile array of clip art.

7. **Roxio Toast.** Even if your material backs up onto a traditional floppy disk, it's a good idea to burn a CD for better data storage. Roxio offers Toast products for you to burn your own CD or DVD, essentially storing data files forever. Available on both PC and Mac.

Note

1. William Strunk, Jr., and E. B. White, *The Elements of Style,* Fourth Edition (Boston: Allyn & Bacon, 2000).

CHAPTER 4

Short Bits, Laugh Lines, and More

Most successful businesses started small. Writing, even for the self-employed, part-time writer, is indeed a business. I can't tell you how many writers set their sights too high when they begin to freelance. Most expect to see their byline in the glossy pages of a four-color magazine. As in other businesses, success generally doesn't happen that swiftly, and they too easily abandon their efforts. It's not until they embrace the concept of "start small, grow big" that they develop a publishing strategy that will see print.

Take a look inside your favorite magazines, newsletters, or even newspapers. Do you see those paragraph-size contributions? How about recent studies or seasonal tips? These overlooked gems are what we call fillers and short bits. If these items are humorous, they qualify as laugh lines. They don't come out of nowhere. They see print because some writer—quite possibly you—understands an editor's need for quick takes on timely topics.

Fillers and short pieces make for fast sales, generating quick cash. When you're published quickly, it does two very important things. It boosts your self-confidence, because now an editor has recognized your potential. Someone has said, "Hey, I like this," and has gone so far as to contact you or requisition a check. This editor has actually opened a door, and if you're smart, you'll recognize the career value offered. In addition, the acquiring editor has validated you financially. Now, don't make plans to leave your day job. Fillers often don't pay much. But who cares? Indeed a $25 sale means as much to the beginning writer as $2,500 does to the contributing editor of an upscale magazine. Some short material pays $100 and beyond.

Why Write Fillers?

Let's pretend you have only one hour daily, and you give yourself weekends off. You could spend each hour crafting a query letter, typing it, revising it, and by Friday, have it printed and in the mail to your favorite magazine. The net effect during your first freelance week is one chance toward acceptance.

If your goal is to write books, you could spend week one researching material and writing an entire chapter of a novel, or perhaps a proposal for a nonfiction book. The net effort effect here isn't even one chance toward acceptance because you haven't completed the work. You'd need the entire novel plus synopsis to sell it, and in nonfiction, you would at least need a sample chapter.

Now, contrast this to the writer who decides to start small. He's done his research, knows a few editors in need of fillers, and each day he's submitted an item to a different editor or market. On Friday, the net effort effect is now five chances toward acceptances. Which writer has the greatest chance toward a self-confident start and monetary validation? If you guessed the five-day, five-way writer, you answered correctly.

You can write several fillers in the amount of time it takes others to produce the first draft of a feature, a chapter in a novel, or even a book proposal. With the possible exception of greeting cards (see Chapter 5), this is your ticket to the quickest cash.

But stacking the odds in your favor isn't the only reason why writing fillers is effective. By consistently producing publishable material, you set yourself up to query editors for larger, better-paying assignments. You become a writer with a name, face, and voice. They'll remember you when you pitch a feature in the months or years to follow. Also, when you finish a longer-length project and sorely need a change of pace, writing a few fillers recharges your creative battery.

Defining a Filler

Short material puts writing to the clear-and-concise test. Let the suggested word count guide you. However, what a magazine editor considers short, a newsletter editor might consider long, but usually, short pieces are defined as being anywhere from 40 to 350 words. Get beyond 300 or 350 words, and you're almost writing a minifeature.

Regardless, you must make each word count. Practice. If your first draft runs long, put it aside. A fresh look the next day allows you to pinpoint a word here or a phrase there that can be cut without sacrificing meaning. Soon you'll tighten the whole piece.

As for content, much of what we read today is service-oriented journalism. It is material that makes the reader healthier, wealthier, wiser, more attractive, better liked, and well adjusted. Fillers and short bits are no different, providing that apprenticeship you'll need for tackling longer-length works later.

Busy readers eat these up because fillers can often be read at a glance and put to use. Editors are always searching for new spins on old topics. In addition, they demand a reason to publish. So if it's not timely (back-to-school tips in August) or service oriented (how the latest study applies to your health), then your filler should be newsworthy. Keep an eye out for studies, research, and interesting angles. If not these three options, try humorous.

Selling Fillers

Most magazines and newspapers buy fillers, and a cursory look through your own favorites will uncover some markets. When studying a publication, it's best to compare bylines with the masthead. If the writer isn't staff, chances are good the piece was freelance written.

Major writing magazines as well as *Writer's Market* and *The Writer's Handbook* list publishers seeking fillers. Realize that although some editors choose not to be included in directories because they're already deluged with incoming mail, they still might be a viable market.

Converting large ideas into succinct bits is another source for filler ideas. Years ago, I interviewed the late children's television host Fred Rogers for a Q&A article. I brainstormed for other angles and the magazines that might feature the material I uncovered. One immediate angle was Idlewild Park in Ligonier, Pennsylvania, home to the only life-size Mr. Rogers' Neighborhood of Make-Believe and a beautiful park for young families to picnic, enjoy rides, and water slides, too. I sold this short bit to a travel magazine, capturing the editor's interest because it was the twenty-fifth anniversary of *Mr. Rogers' Neighborhood* on public television. That served as the news hook. When Mr. Rogers suddenly passed away in 2003, many family-oriented publications sought ways of paying tribute. I resurfaced this theme park for a filler encouraging families to remember his vision.

Don't forget that hints qualify as short bits and so do recipes. You might ask how to test for an idea's originality. Surely if you've heard it then others have also. Exactly. Test the hint on several friends of various ages and genders. Send product-related tips to manufacturers, and send recipe ideas to companies whose ingredients are included. Just find out first whether the company pays for contributions before you share your nifty idea or delicious treat.

Writing Recipes

Years ago, I saw a contest in a woman's magazine that offered tempting cash prizes. The only criterion was to include two cups of a particular cereal. So I set off to learn what it was like to create a recipe.

I brainstormed something useful, something to give as gifts, and something healthy. I wanted to throw as much of this service orientation into one concoction. The end result was a delicious granola recipe my friends and family still devour. Unfortunately, their votes didn't count, because I didn't win a prize. But I went on to publish the recipe in my second book, proving you can often recycle a rejected piece and use it later. What's more important, I learned a lot about writing recipes.

For instance, while I'd always enjoyed granola, I never analyzed it. So I scoured a few cookbooks to see what professionals recommended, and I even read the ingredients on the backs of manufactured products. I picked my favorite ingredients and began experimenting. Of course, it's best to keep a recipe simple, writing with a sequence in mind and a list of ingredients in the order they are needed. There's nothing quite like frustrating a cook with hard-to-find, expensive ingredients. With step-by-step instructions, you won't offend experienced cooks, but by leaving out necessary tips, you will annoy novices. Never use vague measurements such as "a dash of salt." That's too subjective. Stick with specific directions.

Contests that ask you for an essay (in addition to the recipe) are statistically easier to win because few entrants want to bother. Your chances of winning might double. Other tips I've learned from various food writers is that if you change as few as three ingredients from another recipe, you've uniquely stamped your individual signature upon it, and now it's deemed completely new. A fact cannot be copyrighted. In this case, it means the recipe's ingredients and the order in which they're listed and used. Still, make it your own so that it's a new expression of a concept or facts. Copyright does apply to other elements of a recipe or cookbook—that is, captions, explanations, comments, and methods. Obtain permission if you're reprinting for profit and carefully cite the source.

Look to any culinary arts, women's, or parenting magazines, plus newspapers for recipe opportunities. Having said that, men's magazines might also be a market. Be creative, though. Just as you put a new spin on an old topic for fillers, here you can do the same. Magazines for singles and senior citizens run single-serving recipes and tips on easy-to-prepare foods, the college crowd needs to master cooking with a Crock-Pot and hot plate, and religious magazine readers might be adapting recipes to feed large congregations. Meatless, fat-free, or low-cholesterol recipes are relevant for today's readers. If you can make something healthy and make it palatable for children, you've definitely scored big time.

Food, cookware, and appliance companies feature recipes with products, and those Sunday coupon sections feature recipes that may or may not have been created in a corporate test kitchen. Occasionally, greeting card companies feature recipes, especially during holidays. And if you're really blessed by two talents—creating written as well as culinary surprises—ask chefs, restaurants, caterers, nonprofit organizations, or even celebrities who might need help in compiling a cookbook. Point out that by hiring a professional writer, the book will sell more copies, yielding higher profits for everyone involved. If no one of this caliber is available, undertake the role of editor with a community organization compiling a cookbook as a fund-raising project. Sure, you might get paid in book copies, but it will be another credit to promote later. The marketing potential for recipe writing is fabulous as you're not confined to bookstores but can offer demonstrations in grocery or culinary stores as well.

With new dietary findings, and with our busy schedules, the demand for quick culinary magic is not likely to end. Just be sure to test any recipe before it leaves your office. A simple slip, such as using baking soda instead of baking powder, could ruin a recipe. If you're skilled in photography, send along a food photo. You may need to learn some techniques from an experienced food stylist, but a tempting photograph might clinch the sale. In addition, keep up with the trends. Many people prefer to use fresh ingredients.

Because the demand for new recipes and cookbooks has increased, so have the requirements. Cookbooks can no longer tempt readers with mere mouth-watering results. Authors must craft entertaining descriptions, cultural information, and tips for shopping and stocking a well-equipped (and sometimes least expensive) kitchen. Assume your reader has no prior knowledge (or even fondness) for cooking. Of course, you must demonstrate knowledge, as nothing annoys a food editor more than a writer who doesn't know the first thing about cooking.

Every Word Must Work

Whenever you write a filler or recipe, cut right to the action, followed by the results. Use imperative verbs such as "keep," "make," "place," "sprinkle," and "use" to convey the required action. Starting with the verb helps to eliminate unnecessary verbiage. While "stack sweaters on shelves, don't stuff them in drawers" sounds a tad bossy, it gets to the point. Or go one step further with explanation: "Stack sweaters on shelves because stuffing them into drawers doesn't allow the wool to breathe." Start sentences with an infinitive to grab the reader's attention. For instance, "To clear your computer's memory, reboot your machine."

Also, define your problem early on if there's any doubt as to who might care about your tip. To get others to take notice, you might write: "Rudolph might be hungry this winter, but you will be heaping mad if he decides to use your rhododendron as his midnight snack. Purchase deer fence to cover shrubbery this year."

Notice the conditional word "if." The same rule applies to "when." Conditional words help readers grasp your message and mentally make it their own. Finally, write with a sequence in mind. Specific stages help the reader grasp the steps along the way.

Submitting Short Material

We'll talk about pitching longer ideas in letter form in Chapter 6. With fillers being short and often relying on a good tip, humor, or good taste (literally!), you don't need to send a pitch letter or query. Just type your submission in proper manuscript form and submit according to the publication's guidelines. Submit an SASE or a self-addressed, stamped postcard. Some editors prefer e-mail and attached files.

It's not uncommon to wait several weeks for feedback because more than one editor must weigh in with an opinion. If you don't hear back in about four weeks, politely ask about your submission's status. Be prepared to wait longer. Patience pays off, even in the filler market.

Writing for Laughs

For those who remember the 1984 presidential campaign, Ronald Reagan solicited a few chuckles while effectively ending questions about his advanced years. "Age should not be an issue in this campaign," he said. "I will not exploit, for partisan political purposes, my opponent's youth and inexperience."

Whatever your politics, you must admit Reagan won the moment. So can you by crafting punch lines for politicians, public speakers, radio disc jockeys, cartoonists, or publishers. Yes, even editors need filler material that is humorous. *Reader's Digest* is likely the best-known market, and I have it on good authority that it is the publication writers submit to the most. That's a real catch because the odds are still against you with numerous submissions. Realize that *Reader's Digest* isn't the only magazine for your laugh lines. Writing magazines can clue you into potential opportunities along with *Writer's Market* and *The Writer's Handbook*. Don't forget greeting card publishers because most carry a line of funny sentiments (more on this in Chapter 5). If you can put headlines into a humorous light, disc jockeys are always searching for good gags.

Research here includes visiting local comedy clubs as well as watching comedians on television. The same applies to radio and to the morning hosts of radio drive times (the most popular listening hours for radio). Let pop culture and trends be your guides, even presidential elections. When the first President Bush left office, the game of horseshoes was replaced by American fascination with the saxophone (a Clinton pastime). When President Clinton left office, Texas barbecue resurfaced once again after years of joking about Clinton's fast-food habits. Thus, trivia is grist for the humor mill. In fact, many metropolitan newspapers publish a New Year's list of what's in and what's out.

What exactly qualifies as funny? Almost anything, but one of the surest bets in any successful joke is poking fun at yourself or parody. Shared human experience often bonds people together no matter how diverse their backgrounds. It's as if making a confession of your own foibles invites readers (or listeners) to laugh along with you. But beware. We dislike it when others cotton to bullies or glorify tasteless material. While we might laugh at a skit on *Comedy Central* or *Saturday Night Live,* that same material might seem cruel if presented in print. Committing an anecdote to print cements it for us to ponder, and sometimes readers don't like what they read.

The confession of foibles works well to introduce a topic that might otherwise come across as a complaint. For instance, if you're commenting on clever lines you might use with telemarketers, admit that you, too, dislike "dinner-hour interruptus" or share some of the lines you've used, such as "you want Mrs. Smith . . . ah, she's off in Afghanistan." You get the idea.

Exaggeration is another tactic for creating humor. It's not very funny when your two-year-old or teenager whines "you *always* do such and such," but in comedy, if you imitated some powerful figure whining, it might. You might also have the world laughing with you if you compare your stock earnings in a poor economy to the gross national product of a West Virginia mining town. If you deem that line too risky because it's poking fun domestically, try an international spot or loathed individual. Compare inviting your hotheaded brother-in-law over for the holidays with asking Saddam Hussein to Thanksgiving dinner. Humor is often nothing more than drama, just exaggerated.

Stumped for ideas besides yourself and your own anecdotes? Look to children's behavior, home repairs, politics, headline moments, foibles of the rich and famous, even sex as fodder for your next gag. Or make it a combination. Exaggerate your own misfortunes, quirks, biases, or shortcomings. We also laugh at the union of two incongruous things. I'm sure you've heard the much-clichéd phrase by now "nervous like a pregnant nun." That's because the two thoughts don't fit. Often, funny phrases work because of their unpredictability. You've presented one part that the reader/listener expects, and when you surprise them with incongruity, voila—you elicit a laugh.

The writing style for comedy should always err to the concise side because the longer you take setting up the joke, the more the audience expects, thus the greater risk you create if it's not as funny as you presume. Build to that ending. Your punch line is everything. It's the reason for everything preceding it. In fact, make sure you have a powerful punch line before you even start writing. Without this, your joke will surely flop.

Lastly, a sense of rhythm is paramount to good humor writing. We'll discuss this again in Chapter 5, but have you ever wondered why timing works in sets of three? Our brains seem to absorb information best when presented this way. In fact, when presented with a list of four or five data points, most people become overwhelmed with information overload. So three is the writer's lucky number based on brain processing as well as pleasing rhythm. Thomas Jefferson got the concept identifying life, liberty, and the pursuit of happiness while Martin Luther King Jr. repeated a refrain three times: "Free at last! Free at last! Thank God Almighty, we're free at last!"

While your words won't likely find a spot in history books, they can please readers well enough to create a sale—three examples, three anecdotes, three comparisons or exaggerations. Find your own comic perspective, and stick with topics you handle best. If creating something off-color is too far a stretch for you, then stick to what you're most comfortable poking fun at.

Where to Sell Laugh Lines

Local and national comics continually search for fresh, original humor to keep their gigs alive. Since they don't have a lot of time to write their own material, they often turn to freelance joke writers. Public speakers and politicians need these laugh lines just as much. Most metropolitan areas have at least one comedy club where the entertainers might also need a boost of creativity. And, radio personalities also rely on freelance material to make their morning shows wake us up.

Type "comedy network" or "radio network" into an Internet search engine to find outlets. *Comedy USA* publishes an industry guide that lists standup comics and also bookers, club owners, talent coordinators, competitions, and festivals. *The Comedy Market* by Carmine DeSena provides additional ideas and insights into comedic markets. Gene Perret has also written several books on creating comedy as well as numerous compilations of one-liners for toastmasters and public speakers. Refer to the Appendix for appropriate titles.

Advertise your comedy-writing services in professional publications such as *Standup,* the newsletter of the Professional Comedian's Association, which also publishes an annual directory.

In comedy writing, you'll often be paid by the joke or monologue. It's not uncommon for buyers to purchase a few jokes and pass on the rest. If that happens, increase your sales by contributing the rejected jokes to a gag sheet, frequently used by radio personalities. While the pay rate is minimal, you will recoup something for your creative effort. For a listing of gag sheets, check out the market section of *Radio & Records.*

Most laugh lines, jokes, or silly anecdotes are submitted in batches, up to approximately a dozen in each batch. Send each on a separate sheet with your name, address, telephone number, and e-mail on each submission. If you find that your editor prefers electronic submissions, follow that preference.

Creating Puzzles and Brainteasers

Everyone loves a challenge. So if you can't elicit laughs by creating gags and one-liners, you can make readers smile by creating brainteasers and puzzles, carefully manipulating words for potential profit. Software from Variety Games essentially creates the puzzle if you type the list of words.

Study the magazines devoted to puzzles and games. General-interest magazines also feature entertainment with entire pages of crosswords, word searches, word scrambles, and quizzes.

Notice how many publications center their puzzles on a central theme, for instance, nautical terminology or history. Educators even create brainteasers as a way for students to learn vocabulary and key concepts in a fun manner beyond a typical lecture or homework assignment.

Once you have your theme, brainstorm for a list of words pertaining to your subject. Go straight to resource books, jumping to the index for a list of appropriate words. Easily, you can compile a list of hundreds of possibilities—more than you'll need, but fodder for more puzzle projects. Remember to match your pattern of squares to the number run in the magazine. An editor will throw up his hands and throw out your submission if it blatantly exceeds the format.

While puzzles, searches, and scrambles are addictive, so too are quizzes, though judged more harshly. Tempt readers with a reason to complete it. If you sprinkle your quiz with a touch of humor, or some element of intrigue or excitement, you'll be better off than creating a bland quiz without purpose.

Reference Writing

When you research an in-depth topic, where do you turn? Encyclopedias—online or in hefty volumes—provide a wealth of information. That content originated with a writer before it was shaped by an editor. One of those jobs could be yours.

Most encyclopedia companies use experts in the fields of medicine, history, or other specialties. "The name of the game for encyclopedias is authority," says Gary Alt, editorial director of *Encarta*, Microsoft's encyclopedia. Alt has more than thirty years of experience working with the likes of *World Book, Encyclopaedia Britannica,* and *Encarta.* "A body of published work in a particular area is essential," adds Alt. "A science writer who has published by-lined articles in *Science* or *Smithsonian,* or who has authored books on scientific topics, would be considered. Collaborating with an academic author would be a good way of demonstrating the requisite expertise, too." A former managing editor at *Encyclopaedia Britannica* once told me that many husband/wife collaborative writing teams provide content. One has the expertise; the other is better at writing and submitting the material.

So how do you get started in this field? Visit a library with an extensive reference section and study the encyclopedia companies and their styles. Review the contributors' credentials and even employment listings on their Web sites. If after a little research you feel you can compete with academicians who keep up on developments in their fields and ponder the scholarly journals, then write a brief letter of introduction to the editorial director. Send published writing samples; book promotions and releases; and, of course, a résumé or curriculum vitae (CV). If you're a connoisseur of current events, your chances of breaking into the reference-writing market will improve, but be sure to emphasize your expertise in a subject area.

Should you target more than one company? That is truly up to you. The traditional approach would be to offer your expertise to one company at a time, but according to Gary Alt, if a company needs your expertise for a current assignment, where else you've written won't matter that much.

Know what sections of the encyclopedia need to be updated. For instance, if you were a reference writer after the collapse of the World Trade Center, entries on New York would have been revised. Sports writers might be used to compile hundreds of articles on members of the Baseball Hall of Fame. Encyclopedias must stay current.

Encyclopedia yearbooks offer additional opportunities for writers having a flare for magazine article writing only with the subject matter being a scholarly topic. In fact, writing for yearbooks can sometimes pay better than the work in standard reference volumes.

When you write for encyclopedia companies, remember that you are writing for an audience of nonspecialists, not your colleagues. You must limit your esoteric remarks and fully explain the significance of events and ideas. Never assume prior knowledge. Stick to basic principles and developments versus highly technical details.

Many encyclopedias are written for English-reading persons throughout the world, so limit parochialism. Write to achieve universal understanding. Objectivity is also paramount. Always note people's credentials upon first reference when quoting them, explaining their relevance to the subject at hand. Since encyclopedias remain in homes, offices, and libraries for years, try to avoid anything that dates your topic, such as statistics that are likely to change. Eliminate words and phrases such as "recently," "at present," "fifteen years ago," or "just last year."

Writing On-Hold Messages

Though we've all cursed on-hold messages, did you ever wonder who creates these ever-present staples in today's offices? A writer, no doubt. Rather than roll your eyes next time you hear, "We thank you for your patience, all operators are busy helping other customers," why not write something you deem less annoying. Granted, these messages aren't considered high art and they won't make you infinitely wealthy, but they do serve as quick projects for writers wanting to sell their words, build credentials, and bring in some fast cash.

Most clients supply the basic information such as hours of operation and directions and then hire companies to craft their messages. Increase your earnings by thinking creatively. Just as your best bets for fillers center around topical, seasonal, or new solution tips, the same applies to on-hold messages. Beyond "thank you for holding" and "your call is important to us," impart feel-good information about the company, feature trivia or product- or service-related hints, and plant the thought of new purchases. For instance, consumers might forget that every six months they should change the batteries in their smoke detectors. If you're writing an on-hold message for a hardware company, mention this as well as the need to stock up on extra Christmas lights in November, lawn bags in the spring, and an extra propane tank this summer. Hint: Think ahead!

Where to find this plethora of potential clients? Look under "professional" or "general" in classified advertising or type "on-hold messages" into an online directory. When you hear these messages, ask who supplies that company's on-hold tapes. Persistence will pay off when you finally discover the company's name, address, or telephone number. Pay ranges vary, but expect somewhere between $15 and $40 per tape.

Seventy percent of all business calls are placed on hold for the average wait time of nearly one minute, and 90 percent of callers hang up if offered only silence. Therefore, an on-hold message affords a tremendous marketing opportunity for products or services.

Put your best audio-writing skills to the test. If you have a broadcast background, it will help because every word must work, each being the lowest common denominator—that is, skip the fifteen-letter word for the five-letter word that is easier to pronounce and comprehend quickly. Always read your copy aloud. You should time out your scripts with a stop watch because each will be read in a recording studio. Assign male and female roles if necessary, and supply the pronunciation just as you would in writing broadcast copy. You don't want the producers and voice talent to complain about your difficult script.

These scripts span anywhere from a three-minute tape featuring six or eight messages to a six-minute version using between ten and twelve messages. With holidays, seasonal sales, related trivia, company-offered tips, and other events, no doubt there is the chance for constant updating if the client likes your work. Most writers fax drafts to the client and await revisions. Once the client approves changes, plans to record the messages are made. Clients receive new on-hold tapes according to their contracts, but the terms could be monthly, bimonthly, quarterly, or as needed (if some special circumstance develops).

Writers who succeed at this venue say that volume and speed are integral to quick cash. If they can craft a six-minute script in half an hour, they could be making between $30 and $80 an hour.

Trend Appeal

I've discussed the importance of spotting trends, but it's so vital to the sale of short pieces, fillers, and even greeting cards that it bears repeating. The best trend-spotting publications are metropolitan newspapers such as *USA Today* and *American Demographics* and current books by trend-reporting authors such as Faith Popcorn. Type "trends" into the search field on a bookseller's Web site to yield a myriad of current resources.

Voracious reading and staying abreast of emerging technology, future predictions, and pop culture pays off. This way, you'll understand the heady influence of hot new products, movies, and television programs. You'll know what music people are listening to, and whether there is a new dance craze sweeping the nation. Knowledge of current events helps you to predict political, financial, and social changes. Seminars and conferences identify key speakers, breaking research, or even new products. Trade shows and conventions do likewise.

The key here is keeping ahead of trends and, ultimately, using these to your advantage as you see them emerge and evolve.

Adapt your creative strategies as well as your ideas and submissions. Consider trends the gold that you, the savvy writer, should mine successfully.

If you transfer your writing skills into communications endeavors such as public relations, marketing, and advertising, trends are equally important when working with clients, developing campaigns, and coming out ahead of one's competitors.

Starting-Out Steps

Writing for quick cash is nowhere more apparent than in the creation of short material, fillers, hints, humor, laugh lines, recipes, puzzles, messages, and even reference copy. The need is great, and the more prolific you become, the more money you can stash into your bank account. That validates you as a professional, and the fast sale bolsters your self-confidence. When starting out, you should:

- Look to publisher guidelines and writing magazines for markets accepting fillers, laugh lines, brainteasers, puzzles, and more.
- Pay attention to trends—the foundation of fillers, salable recipes, and humorous gags. Keep abreast of current events and change for use in reference writing or editing.
- Consider collaborating with scholarly individuals who lack the writing experience you offer. Together, you'd make a great team for online or print encyclopedia companies, where demonstrated expertise is critical.
- Craft on-hold messages using your ability to plan ahead, think creatively, and draft a broadcast-quality script to market products or services.
- Hone a clear and concise writing style. Make every word count. Test your final recipe, tip, or joke before submitting. Read your on-hold messages aloud.
- Think ahead, think seasonally, and sell ideas accordingly.

CHAPTER 5

Greeting Cards and Poetry

According to the Greeting Card Association (GCA) based in Washington, D.C., 7 billion greeting cards are bought annually with retail sales totaling $7.5 billion. That is a 20 percent increase over figures reported in 1993.

In classes I've taught, I've often included greeting card writing because it's a fun, money-making endeavor, accomplished in small increments of time. Most of my students light up. Okay, a few men choose this opportunity to sneak out as they fail to see how it applies to them. Many students—men or women—had no previous knowledge that creating heartfelt sentiments and zany expressions could generate income. Someone needs to channel these sudden sparks of inspiration into the text that appears on cards and gift-giving products. It might as well be you.

Giftware and greeting card verses can be conceived just about anywhere—as you sit at red lights during your morning commute, commiserate with coworkers over lunch, or watch TV at night. If you keep a journal of ideas, these serve as fodder for your next verse.

How Does Poetry Fit?

Poetry is not the easiest form of writing to sell. If you're a poet, this is no surprise. Poems might find a home in collections produced by small presses or online magazines. Commercial publishers might occasionally produce a book of poems, but not often enough to make serious money, I'm afraid.

Plenty of literary magazines may publish your poems, but if making money is your primary objective, you might want to shift your writing style into the greeting card industry. That's why I included poetry in this chapter to give you more sales opportunities. If you want to maintain the integrity of and pride in your poetry, keep pursuing the markets. Books like *Poet's Market* by Writer's Digest and Jeff Mock's *You Can Write Poetry* can become important sales tools. If you're open to other possibilities, stay with this chapter.

Bear in mind that an immediate turnoff to editors, however unfair you deem this prejudice, occurs when a writer requests to place and sell his poems. That is because greeting card editors don't really consider their editorial product to be poetry. In traditional poetry, poems are the vehicle for the writer's unique self-expression. Greeting cards, on the other hand, express the sentiments of thousands through the creator. You, as writer, act as a conduit.

Industry Background

In the 1800s, you went to the local dry goods store where the clerk showed you available sentiments, inserting your choice into blank cards. Calligraphy may or may not have been used. Then in the 1870s, Louis Prang—who some call the "father of the American Christmas card"—pasted sentiments onto calendars. He became the first to mass-produce greeting cards, and today, the GCA recognizes his influence with its "Louie" Awards, announced each May. The Louie Award is the greeting card equivalent of the Oscar. It's no small contest. The 2002 awards had eighty different categories, judged on imagination, emotional impact, artistry, ability to sell, and the harmony struck between the card's visual elements and verse. Awards are presented at a gala affair, and top-winning cards are usually featured on network morning shows and in other publicity.

J. C. Hall and Jacob Saperstein purveyed their greeting cards in pushcarts during the early 1900s. The convenience of using someone else's sentiments appealed to Americans, and soon Hallmark and American Greetings were founded. Incidentally, these companies still are the largest industry players.

By 1941, the GCA opened its doors. With servicemen and servicewomen off in World War II, the industry grew as devout family and friends used the newly emerging cards to send their best wishes and encouragement. The Vietnam era did the same.

Whether flower children of the 1960s or Ali McGraw and Ryan O'Neil in *Love Story* spawned it we're not sure, but in the 1970s, greeting cards became much more romantic and softer sounding. In the years that followed, the energy and hostage crises occurred as well as illnesses and addictions being freely acknowledged by many Americans, including public figures. Realism crept into greeting cards. Divorce was no longer a taboo topic. A sentiment along the lines of "welcome back from rehab" might have actually sold. According to the GCA, that relaxed attitude—today manifesting in casual Fridays and reaching out via the Internet—continues to permeate, paving the way for nonoccasion and encouragement cards as well as a breezy conversational tone. However, no matter how fast paced our society has become, emotions remain the driving force behind many people's motivations and actions. Greeting cards can offer the antidote for a sagging spirit. If you can think of your work as a real emotional boost when people need it most, you're doing much more than adding income and accomplishment to your career.

As you can imagine, my push toward becoming a trend watcher still applies in this chapter. Greeting cards reflect American life. In fact, the GCA reports that everyday card-sending situations such as birthday, anniversary, get well, sympathy, encouragement, and others account for half of all retail sales whereas holiday cards comprise the other 50 percent. What's more, you must look at the entire sentiment-bearing market for potential money-making opportunities.

Sandra Louden, a greeting card writer who wrote a Louie Award–winning caption for Current, Inc., has worked in this industry for nearly twenty years. She made her first sale after three months of perseverance and today has sold hundreds of sentiments and self-published *Write Well & Sell: Greeting Cards*. Louden's captions also appear on calendars and miscellaneous giftware.

Income Potential

Greeting card writing truly qualifies as a fast-cash prospect. Top companies pay the most ($100 to $200 per verse), but of course, your competition is much steeper there. Hundreds of companies pay $10 to $100 for a conventional or traditional verse. If you're selling humor or longer material, you can usually count on a bigger check of perhaps $40 to $300.

Writers who hear these rates are typically thrilled, except that the industry pays no royalties. Unless you're so successful that you license popular material (such as Dilbert or Cathy), it's standard to sell all rights. But we're talking about a sentence or two—in most cases, that is the typical length. You may bristle at giving up rights, but imagine the company if it didn't operate this way. It would pay for a verse and spend a lot of money to emblazon it onto cards, T-shirts, or calendars. Then you could turn around and sell it to another vendor to put on similar merchandise. Not a good way to conduct business. Having presented the company side, I'll advocate for writers as well. If your material is lengthy, consider its potential as a minibook or even a children's book with a book publisher. Sell all rights as a greeting card only if you've exhausted this possibility.

Before accepting any material, a greeting card editor will likely send you a disclosure form stating that the material you submit is original. Sign and return it promptly. After you sell specific verses, more paperwork follows for that specific caption.

Types of Greeting Cards

Before going much further, we need to understand the types of cards editors seek. *Traditional* or *conventional cards* are the best known. They often feature rhymed or metered verse. These are the sentimental favorites, the cash cows in one sense, allowing these companies to introduce new lines. Mostly written by staff writers, traditional cards focus on seasonal occasions such as Christmas, Valentine's Day, Mother's Day, and Father's Day.

Contemporary cards feature prose, much realism, and little to no rhyme involved. These are often conversational in tone, as if you're witnessing a caring conversation between two friends. They can even take on the role of cheerleading. *Studio cards* are humorous greetings reflecting everyday life. These are sometimes on the cutting edge of humor, and you might characterize them as "off the wall."

Finally, *alternative cards* use both humor and contemporary prose as they reflect life, frequently dealing with single parenting, coping, stepfamilies, job loss, terminal illness, the environment, addiction, and other modern circumstances. These cards didn't exist in the 1960s or early 1970s when excessive sentiment ruled. Sandra Boynton changed all that in 1974 with a clever, alternative approach, designing and writing cards to pay her Yale tuition bills. By 1980, Boynton cards sold 80 million cards annually. She truly recognized societal changes that made alternative cards appropriate to send.

Knowing What Is Needed

What is salable today is not necessarily what sold fifteen or twenty years ago. Today's editors purchase material that reflects current needs. The messages are more finely tuned. "Thinking of you" has transformed into "thinking of you because your pet died" or "thinking of you because I know you're a great kid, trying hard."

Visiting different gift shops, bookstores, grocers, pharmacies, and party supply stores is no doubt the best way to research card companies and verses. Internet research is helpful, but nothing replaces being

Stuck for Ideas?

If you're searching for new ideas, remember the most common themes in greeting cards include the following:

- Gratitude and appreciation
- Best wishes
- Love and affection
- Sharing memories
- Cheerleading
- Toasting or congratulating
- Remembering the recipient on specific occasions
- Thinking of the recipient in illness, stress, sympathy, or for no reason at all

able to physically read the card and turn it over, because the back side often contains useful information for writers. Look at the range of verses and the various lines of products. Don't limit your search. Mail-order companies specialize in cards, posters, mugs, T-shirts, note pads, and beverage napkins. Seek out the serious, the silly, the risqué, the religious, and everything in between.

Greeting card companies publish writer's guidelines and needs lists, especially once you begin working with particular editors. Request guidelines by writing to each company with an SASE or, more efficiently, look on the Internet. *Writer's Market* and *The Writer's Handbook* also offer guidelines.

If you know very little about the greeting card industry, know this: Women purchase 90 percent of all cards. Molly Wigand, author of *How to Write & Sell Greeting Cards, Bumper Stickers, T-Shirts and Other Fun Stuff*, once gave me a great tip for male writers in this business. "Except when otherwise noted," she said, "You are a woman!" Indeed the ability to think like a woman; empathize with others; and tap into the feelings of love, friendship, sadness, sorrow, joy, and elation are all prerequisites for a career in greeting card writing. Let's face it: I don't know many men who send each other cards in cheer-up mode as women customarily do.

This is probably why men sometimes exit when I address greeting cards in my classes. But one male student, in particular, impressed me when he came to class after having researched various greeting card guidelines. Finding companies that wanted humor and off-color captions, he had a novel way of meeting that need. "I figure I can take my golf buddies out for a drink," he said. "That's gotta be good for a dozen captions right there!" Now this man was thinking creatively, not letting gender stereotypes deter his ability to make money. I've seen many husbands and wives or girlfriends and boyfriends take my writing classes. If I were part of such a duo, I'd work as a team because men and women bring different sensibilities to their writing. Together, they can both succeed at greeting cards.

Turning Ideas into Verses

All captions begin as ideas. That is why keeping a journal is a very practical and very wise thing to do. Often, it comes down to word association and brainstorming. One helpful exercise is to write different occasions for sending cards such as new baby, wedding, and woman-to-woman friendship atop a blank sheet of paper. Make it into columns. Under each, list as many words as you can associate with the category. Write everything, dismissing nothing. Your goal is to get a range of emotions, words, and phrases to work with.

When I started this book, memories of my remarriage were still fresh. I looked through the basket of cards my husband and I received. Some key words and phrases were "congratulations"; "dreams come true"; "lifetime"; "happiness"; "two hearts"; "two minds"; "love grown deeper"; "soul mate"; "deserve each other"; "beautiful blessings"; "God's planning"; "magic moments"; "two becoming one"; as well as "faith," "hope," and "love." I found Scripture too, with I Corinthians 13:13, of course, but also verses such as Ecclesiastes 3:1, which stated, "There is a right time for everything."

You can see the range of captions—everything from the religious and sentimental to something lighter, more humorous. Think of all words, phrases, imagery, and potential meanings.

Another exercise to provoke ideas is putting a new spin on an old problem. Pretend you're writing a woman-to-woman friendship caption. Children have always been a challenge to entertain but years ago there were no video games, VCRs, or DVDs. Same problem, different solution. Greeting cards reflect the culture in which we live. Meet the challenges life presents us, only in a different way.

Look at a subject from the opposite perspective. After all, some savvy creators took a dinosaur (typically a threatening creature in children's eyes) and transformed him into a purple singing-and-dancing sensation. Do the same with other ideas. Just remember that regardless of your technique, you must convey a greeting. No greeting, no sale.

Draw upon your own circumstances, gaining sensitivity to create powerful messages. Take yourself back to the innocent child bursting with the thought of Christmas. If you've gone through some difficult life passages, such as divorce, grieving the death of a loved one, or loss of a job, try to unearth those raw emotions. What helped you through? Life's sorrows can increase our capacity for compassion. My own journey through divorce inspired me to research a book enabling others to also turn loss into opportunity. *Surviving Separation and Divorce* resulted, and one of the best reviews was from a woman who said reading it lifted a huge burden from her shoulders. Perhaps a similar struggle will inspire a great caption from you and provide an emotional boost to someone in need.

Me-to-You Messages

Connecting with recipients is what it's all about—that is, connection in a global yet personal kind of way. Remember the sixth "W" of journalism: "Who cares?" You must have enough recipients who can relate to your sentiment, but when they open that card, they'll also feel it was written specifically for them. This is what we call a "me-to-you message."

A me-to-you message can be funny, but it should never be a tease that is a disguised dig. There should never be mean intent or political, ethnic, or sensitive subject matter. Write to build up, not tear down. Test your humor on a variety of friends if you're uncertain how a particular caption will be taken. If you get stuck creating me-to-you messages, write down what you're trying to convey without the right words, rhyme, or meter. Work it until it flows.

Other Caption Construction

Just as in crafting gags, the power of three is evident in creating captions. The human brain seems to best accept information broken down into three parts. For example, for a business congratulations card, you could write, "Three little words every businessperson loves to hear . . . It's tax deductible!" Obviously, those three words could be the inside verse, followed by congratulations on your new venture or some other greeting. Divide verses for the proper comedic effect, enough to deliver a laugh or a groan without giving

---

Example: Humorous Love Caption

After all these years, I've discovered our love consists of three things: Spending time with you after long, hard days; sharing your deepest thoughts and heartfelt concerns; and . . . helping you find virtually everything you ever look for: But I love that too!

away the punch line in the outside verse or first-second parts. What if you don't have three levels of inspiration? Invent some! Take an example from real life and stretch it to fit the format.

Two additional ways to communicate a message include drawing comparisons and reworking a phrase or a cliché. Riddles and rhymes, if you're skilled at using these techniques, offer even more caption construction options. Rhyme and meter can enhance a me-to-you message, or it can get in the way. If you can make it move, that is great, but don't force the meter. Allow the accent to fall on the syllable it would naturally fall on in everyday speech.

Bible verses are sometimes required as the inspiration of religious captions. If your verse reflects a specific Biblical passage, be sure to cite the chapter and verse as well as the translation you used.

In *You Can Write Greeting Cards*, Karen Ann Moore urges writers to deepen the connection between the card sender and recipient. Take a verse you've crafted and be even more direct, more specific. Start with a fact, such as "It's your birthday . . ." and build the sentiment around that fact, or even a problem—and if you're getting older, there is a definite pun/problem there. Finally, try techniques such as alliteration ("She sells seashells by the seashore"), literary inspiration (taking a great first sentence and expanding with a verse that is fresh and new), or the use of surprise (romantic promise on outside, something silly inside).

Formatting and Submitting Verses

First, company guidelines supersede any protocol I extol here. The traditional way of submitting verses has been on 3-by-5-inch index cards (without lines). In the illustration provided, you'll see that you must devise a coding concept at the top left corner. You can use your initials, a code for the occasion (such as "B" for birthday or "TY" for thank you), or perhaps the first three letters of the company where you submit. For instance, "CUR" could stand for Current Inc. Be optimistic as you code and number. Make it "B-001" with the thought that you'll have hundreds of submissions. You might even say such a technique also makes you look quite prolific at first glance.

Most cards have both an outside and inside verse, though some have only one. An "O:" stands for the outside verse and what follows, and an "I:" stands for inside verse and its contents.

Sandwiched between your code and your outside verse might be a graphic idea as depicted in the illustration. Mind you, editors aren't obligated to use your graphic idea. In fact, I once proposed a cruise ship for a travel or vacation card, and when I got the finished product, the company had used my verse on a thinking-of-you card with a cat on the cover peering out a window at a sailboat. By all means, if you feel your art concept could sell the verse, go ahead and include it. Just know that your editor may see things differently.

> **Format Illustration**
>
> **MJR-001** (*Happy Birthday—Grandmother*)
> (**OUTSIDE GRAPHIC:** Grandma in tennis shoes soaring down sidewalk on scooter)
> **I:** *Having another birthday certainly hasn't slowed you down.*
> Example courtesy Mary Jo Rulnick/Palm Press.

Submit six to twenty cards in a batch, accompanied by an SASE (you'll want to receive the rejected captions for your records). For longer material, standard paper is fine, one submission per page, mailed flat. A cover letter isn't necessary, unless you want to briefly introduce yourself.

Proofread your cards and correspondence. Everything should appear neat and orderly. For writers who live off their laser output, don't despair. Avery makes index cards for you to insert into a laser printer, but I would advise you to run a test copy so as not to waste this more expensive card stock while aligning things correctly.

Frequent Mistakes Beginners Make

What is the difference between buying your cards from Current Inc. and visiting your local grocery store to pick out a verse?

There is a huge difference, in fact. Companies have found that consumers who actually walk up to a card counter do so with an intended person and occasion in mind. That motivation differs drastically from catalog or Web site purchases simply to have cards on hand for impromptu use.

So what? Well, if you as a writer send the wrong verses to the wrong companies, it brands you as ignorant of the industry. Take anniversaries, for example. Your local rack probably features a general anniversary card, as well as happy first anniversary, celebrating a silver anniversary, and happy fiftieth anniversary cards. That is four different kinds of anniversary cards for a retail-driven card company. But your catalog- or Internet-based retailer may only feature a general, one-size-fits-all anniversary product. Likewise, send a "thank-you-to-the-teacher" card to Current Inc., and don't be surprised by the rejection. It's too specific. Save these ideas for the point-of-purchase companies.

Another mistake that beginning writers fall victim to is letting one editor's rejection squash their creativity. With any rejection, it helps to know why you were rejected, and if the editor scrawls on her reply that the company already had similar material, you know it at least wasn't you or your efforts. Send it to other companies. Heed any advice you're given. Perhaps by changing only a word or two, you can increase your chances of a quicker sale upon your next submission. Never underestimate the power of the rewrite, if that is what it takes.

Patience is also a necessary commodity. Some editors will return a set of rejected captions, yet hold on to others for months, routing them to colleagues for their feedback. In fact, many beginners fail to realize that it's collective opinion that counts. Your job is to turn one editor on to your caption. That editor, in turn, takes it to a meeting or circulates it in the department.

While editors are making their decisions—which could take months, unfortunately—keep your creative energy alive. Send off another batch to another company. But don't submit the same captions to multiple companies because this is a surefire way to alienate two editors who may end up each wanting to purchase the same verse. The end result will be alienation among both editors. No writer needs that.

Finally, I realize how wonderful it would be to find your work showcased at your local Hallmark shop. The odds are against you, however; and I've seen students set their sights too high, get hit by rejection, and give up. Don't let that be you. Set realistic goals with the hundreds of smaller companies.

Increasing Your Chances of Success

The best way to keep the income flowing is to do a consistently good job for your editors, build relationships with them, and encourage them to review additional work. Keep abreast of their needs by e-mailing and phoning occasionally. Request an updated needs list as this shows you want to help them, not just further your own money-making mission.

While greeting card writers are not required to submit artwork, the more visual you can think, the more money you will make. Fail to at least consider this facet of greeting card production, and your editor will see it as a sign of weakness. If you can offer complete writing/ illustration packages and your own line of products, you may even be able to strike a more favorable contract or choose to self-publish your work. But don't be surprised if the company you submit to already has a working stable of illustrators and photographers.

Brainstorm the possibilities for posters, bumper stickers, mugs, T-shirts, note pads, sticky notes, beverage napkins, plaques, and more. A whole array of giftware and paper goods depends on creative writers. I submitted "coupons for new moms" as a gift product many years ago, and the merchandise coordinator at Current Inc. had just returned from maternity leave. Talk about fortuitous. It went into the next catalog.

Starting-Out Steps

Remember, in our busy world, you can be the conduit of feelings that other people long to express. Just think of the sheer power some sentiments have. After reading this chapter, you could run out to the office supply store (for a typewriter, a stack of index cards, a journal, and some envelopes), the post office (for stamps), and the bookstore (for resources with guidelines and perhaps a rhyming dictionary). You could be in business in only a few short hours. If you already own a computer with Internet access, you're one step ahead. Little overhead and readily available ideas almost 24/7 make this a particularly enjoyable encounter. Keep in mind the following tips:

- Spot trends and keep current. Scour magazine advertisements, product catalogs, and even the newspapers to get a pulse on what is hot and what is not.

- Consider other avenues for your poetry. Captions might be a different way of thinking initially, but you may find that editors could use your talents.

- Visit greeting card companies online, viewing their Web sites for guidelines and sample captions.

- Keep a journal of ideas. Cultivate the talent of thinking visually so that there is enough imagery for your editor, an illustrator, or a photographer to do the rest.

- Recycle rejected captions. If they continue to meet rejection, analyze them. Perhaps they lack universal appeal, or a me-to-you message, and need to be repackaged for successful sale.

- Don't forget self-expression products as a way of making more money with your captions. These include Post-it® Notes, calendar or mug captions, T-shirt slogans, or bumper-sticker phrases.

- Realize that this is a work-for-hire industry, for the most part. You will relinquish all rights to your verses, unless otherwise stated.

CHAPTER 6

Query Letters and Article Submissions

"YOU MEAN I SHOULDN'T JUST WRITE THE ARTICLE AND SEND IT IN?" Usually such petitions are uttered from beginning writers with a true "say it isn't so" tone, but my reply is standard. "Yep, that's right," I'll say, sometimes describing the height of the typical slush pile at most magazines, and why editors prefer a streamlined approach. Later in this chapter, I'll discuss the specifics of approaching newspaper editors.

This say-it-isn't-so dismay stems from the beginner's desire to publish the article she's conceived and labored over—her baby in a sense, as it often carries that significance. She's not only married to the idea, but convinced that Article X belongs in Magazine Y. If this writer has carefully reviewed the magazine and contributor guidelines, more power to her. However, many new writers approach a magazine based on preconceived notions that sometimes aren't rooted in the publication's true identity. In fact, as they submit material, some writers dare to argue, thinking they just know their piece is perfect for the lineup, that even though the guidelines say "no first-person pieces," their story will *surely* place a smile on the editor's face. How about a frown! No means no. Rare is the writer with the power to change formats.

Studying a Publication

There are professional caveats in publishing. One is that editors know their magazines better than any writer could ever hope to know them.

Another is that editors want a hand creating content because they also know their readers' profile. Studying the magazine (or newspaper) helps writers to research this content and profile.

A magazine's cover tells you what is important. In fact, conceive all queries or article ideas as cover lines. Editors place enticing teasers on covers to grab your attention. These lines shout "Buy me!" from across the grocery store. Incorporate numbers into your pitches whenever possible. Promise the reader something that sizzles. You don't need to look far on certain covers to see what is on the hot list of topics: sex, saving money, dieting, more sex, and six best ways to (do whatever). You get the idea.

Next, study the advertisements because advertisers pay top dollar for them. You can be certain they're getting a return on that investment if you see repeat advertising, and this gives us a glimpse into the lifestyle and products used by magazine readers. It tells us how to make our ideas relevant to our readers. Please don't pitch an idea on "top-ten bargain vacations" to a magazine featuring Mediterranean cruises, Lexus automobiles, and Rolex watches. Similarly, while new parent or self-employed magazines might appreciate a rundown of tax tips, the same idea is altogether inappropriate for a journal targeting accountants who should already know this.

Other items to scrutinize include the table of contents in order to find standing departments and what items are features. Scour the editor's column, gleaning some connection with this person (maybe you have children the same ages, the same home town or alma mater) or a hint as to the editorial direction and what is important. Then, study contributor biographies, looking to see whether you're in the league of other featured writers. If you're not, wait until you've culled enough exposure in other magazines or newspapers. Compare bylines with a magazine masthead. If you don't see the writer's name, it's fair to assume the person a freelancer. This is a positive sign. Of course, read the magazine as thoroughly as possible and, in particular, the department you've targeted. Ideally, you want to study six to twelve months of recent back issues to get a true feel for the publication. Beg, borrow, and preferably don't steal these issues, but ask others to save their magazines, make friends with receptionists in waiting rooms (especially ask if they get multiple copies), and fork out the money for your own subscription. Compare your notes to the contributor guidelines as published on the magazine's Web site or within *Writer's Market* or *The Writer's Handbook,* resources that print thousands of guidelines as well as the percentage of freelance material purchased. In addition, you'll find whether the magazine pays upon acceptance or publication. You hope for the former because the latter means you'll wait months, sometimes years, for a paycheck.

Crafting a Query Letter

The query letter is the industry-accepted approach of contacting magazine editors and pitching ideas. To query means to ask, thus this pitch to an editor. Make that a specific editor with a name that you've verified as being the most appropriate person to receive your idea. Query letters introduce you to the editor and hook him or her into wanting your topic. They do this by presenting real fact nuggets of information, an outline of how you'd handle the topic, who you'd interview, and your credentials as a writer. A good query letter answers: "Why should I care?"; "Why should I assign this article to you?"; "What take-away value will my reader obtain?"; and sometimes "Does this fit with our editorial calendar, proposed themes, or advertising this issue?"

Query letters represent your writing ability so the skill of persuasive writing is paramount. This letter, however, should never—ever—begin with "Enclosed please find a query about . . ." No style there. No persuasion either. Depending on your topic, you might decide to persuade with a straightforward, direct summation of fact and introduction of experts who will offer commentary. This works well when you're alerting your editor of a startling statistic as the compelling reason to publish. Here's a variation of a query I've submitted to parent-related magazine editors:

> Approximately one out of every five Americans has an anger problem, and unfortunately, children are not excluded from these numbers. A single outburst doesn't make an angry child. However, left unchecked, anger does signal a problem. Many parents would love to point to society's ills or some chemical imbalance as the source, and while these factors may be the cause, it's also empowering for parents to learn ways they can help their children.

As author of *The Angry Child,* Dr. Tim Murphy, a psychologist and congressman, says, "The good news is that if family is part of the problem, they have the power to become part of the solution as well." Dr. Murphy has identified four types of family behaviors that can actually add to a child's anger, even in families that seem to have it all going well on the surface. More importantly, he knows how these families can help their out-of-sorts child onto a happier life track. In a feature for your magazine, . . .

Surprise, and even using fiction techniques and dialogue, can work. In the fall of 2002, if this (fictitious) scenario began your query, you'd have gotten most editors to set down their coffee:

When my brother calls me, it's usually no big deal. But this Thursday in October was quite another thing. Everyone around the Washington metro area had some raw nerves, especially careful about where they pumped gas. Some wouldn't even go out for groceries for fear of being a victim of the DC sniper, so my brother's call woke me with a bit of worry.

Of course, I'd heard the sniper description I informed him as he rambled away. We were all watching the news 24/7. "Is this why you called me at 5 A.M.," I asked through a yawn.

"No sis," he replied, "I was chatting with the sniper guy in a restaurant just last night!"

This would qualify as a shocking coincidence pegged to a nation-wide news story, using dialogue to get to the point. Another approach would be a question such as "Remember when . . . ?" or "Have you ever needed gas in your car and thought nothing of driving up to the pump?" Regardless of the approach, a case like this demands an e-mail or faxed query—even if the guidelines state postal mail preferred. Editors treat breaking news with different standards, and so should we.

A query is also succinct, ideally one page (never more than two), sometimes with bullets to help the editor follow your thought process as you build your idea into a possible feature. Stick to one topic at a time, and propose no more than two different, detailed ideas in each query letter. No laundry lists please. These overwhelm the editor and paint you as an amateur.

If you're a writer who has that article already written, please don't dash off a hasty letter just because I told you this is the accepted approach. Really spend time crafting a convincing argument to publish your idea because in today's climate, it's as if editors are searching for reasons not to publish your work. Remember my sixth "W": Who cares? Make your editor care. Going one step further, what is the expected outcome? Will reading your article make a person healthier, wealthier, wiser, happier, fulfilled, or more attractive? Will it satisfy a thirst for the topic of the day?

Query letters offer a complete concept in the format of a typewritten business letter. If you think there is ancillary information to help readers grasp a concept—such as charts, photographs, illustrations, sidebars, or subheadings—this is the time to mention it. In fact, suggest that you could write a sidebar in addition to the article since it may actually net you a larger paycheck. Just be careful to study the magazine well. If you always spot a sidebar as part of a particular feature package then producing one may be expected of you and already included in the overall freelance fee. When negotiating a rate or contract amount, politely ask if sidebars pay extra. If you don't ask, you definitely won't earn more money.

Speak up and tout whatever credentials set you apart. A query letter never advertises your lack of experience. If you were the editor and a writer said, "I've never written for publication before, but I'd love to appear in your magazine . . ." would that line instill confidence in you?

If you struggle to answer why you're the best person to write the feature, then choose another topic. There must be some compelling reason that you're querying—your vocation and stellar knowledge, personal experience, advanced study, books and extensive research, a lifelong hobby or passion, fate or circumstance—something that gives you an edge. Sad to say, but editors know that the research and writing prowess of new writers doesn't equal that of veterans in the magazine's stable of writers. At least one credential must stand out.

One way for newcomers and established writers alike to showcase their credentials is to craft a one-page bio to send with each query. List publications and articles about to appear in print (with the most prestigious taking center stage), educational background, public speaking or teaching experiences, media interviews, memberships, and maybe a few lines of personal description. If being the mother of six boys could help to sell a first-person account of understanding the male psyche, you could even customize a few lines. If you've won awards for your cooking, that fact matters to the editor of *Food & Wine*. Being a greeting card writer counts if you're selling humor or even editing your church newsletter when you have little work-related experience to include.

At the same time, find a reason why the editor should consider your topic now. If you know that recently enacted tax legislation is set to take effect in a few months, query an editor about how the new laws affect day-to-day decisions in most families. Now there's a news peg. If your editor has requested a query, use a stamp marked "requested material" on the outside of your envelope, but only do so if the package is in fact expected. You can get a stamp like this made at your local office supply store.

Query letters are written for one editor at a time. Editors frown upon simultaneous submissions. Have a list of other possible markets ready if you are turned down. Finally, your query letter should always ask for the assignment. A simple phrase such as "If this idea fits with your editorial plans, I hope you'll assign the article to me" is all that's required, but amazingly, it shows a little initiative. That is another trait that will set you apart from other aspiring writers. Always include pertinent clippings (keep reading for further details) as well as some response vehicle for the editor's decision (an SASE or self-addressed stamped postcard). I've found that the postcard gets better results because it's much easier to reply to questions you pose on the card. On my postcards, I've included the article idea, magazine, and my name at the top. I handwrite this or I type it onto a 3-by-5-inch prestamped postcard (available at the post office). Then I make a line with a check-off space for "keeping and considering," "sorry cannot use because _____," and occasionally as the last bullet, "please submit again." That blank line after the word "because" is very important, and in my unscientific survey, I find it grants the writer some comfort with the explanation.

Selecting Appropriate Clippings

Clips or tear sheets prove that you're a published writer. Choose clips that represent the type of query you're sending. If you're pitching a health topic, choose health-related work. Starting out, you'll have a limited selection. If that is the case, or if you lack any clips, be certain that you can answer the question "Why should I assign this to you?" because then your background and everything else you offer truly must get you the assignment. As time passes, you'll have more prestigious clips to offer.

When I moved my home office, I hadn't had the luxury of tossing out years' worth of files, including clips I'd saved since I began freelancing. I smiled uncovering some early samples. While tossing these into the recycle bin, I was humbled to remember just how much they meant twenty years prior. You'll feel this way, too, someday.

Because this industry thrives on presentation, it's best to mail your clips in a flat envelope so that they appear neat and unfolded, along with your typewritten query letter. Paperclip or staple your business card to these clips. Type a label and neatly affix it on the outside. Make sure that you've placed sufficient postage. Nothing cements a poor impression faster than "postage due."

Sample Query Letters

In his book *Queries & Submissions*, Thomas Clark shares extensive advice. Realizing the purpose of the query is to propose an article, show idea development, grab an editor's attention, introduce credentials, and present a working title, Clark shared what I consider to be a classic pitch he once made to *Modern Bride:*

Shortly before the wedding day, my soon-to-be mother-in-law fixed me with a stare from across the dinner table. "No mother-in-law jokes, OK?" Our good rapport over the seven years since has only partially been due to my honoring her request. And the few major disagreements have come when I forgot "The Key to Getting 'In' With Your In-Laws." I'll reveal that key in . . .[1]

Of course, it helped that Clark chose an evergreen topic, but he fit all requirements into the first paragraph. Below, I've tried to paint word pictures that most travel (or even health) editors could at least imagine themselves in, with this query opening:

> Your flight pulls away from the gate in three hours, and the airport shuttle is set to arrive in thirty minutes. You've made all the necessary transit arrangements, or so you think. While you mentally check off your packing list, have you thought about your primary mode of transportation while sightseeing, shopping, and meandering about? I don't mean taxicabs here. I'm talking about your feet! Pack the wrong kind of shoes, and sightseeing might just turn into hobbling. In fact, the first step you take some morning could be met with a sharp pain that could permanently ruin your travel outings for some time.
>
> I know. As I cavalierly tossed flat shoes into my suitcase, thinking they'd be comfortable, I unknowingly set the stage for conditions that would later be diagnosed as plantar fasciitis and heel spurs, the most common ailments driving patients to podiatrists. In an article for . . .

Beyond the basics, if you remember one thing about crafting a winning query, let it be this—create interest. Make your reader want to know more about your idea. If you can help the reader to insert himself or herself and circumstances into your topic, great. But if that doesn't work, at least make it compelling enough to arouse empathy, spark curiosity, and perhaps create the best scenario of all in "I've got to see where this is leading." If you get your editor that far, you'll know you've mustered what it takes to write a convincing query.

Following Up Queries

If weeks pass, and your trusty reply card, envelope, or e-mail has not arrived in your mailbox, it's time to be proactive. I wait at least four weeks before I place a telephone call or send an e-mail, unless what I sent is so timely that it warrants quick turnaround. This may seem an inordinate amount of time, but you must remember that decisions are made slowly in publishing. Typically, it's not up to only one editor to decide what content falls with the publication's pages. Thus, it takes time to obtain that colleague feedback.

E-mail follow-up is often preferable because it's less of an interruption. You can read it when you choose as opposed to a phone call that could catch an editor in the middle of a deadline.

The possible responses you may hear include some standard rejection lines, but editors may also offer another closely related assignment. If your editor has taken the time to pass along a personal comment, pay attention. If an editor requests more data, it shows a level of interest, perhaps to justify to colleagues why your idea is great. It could very well be your editor saying "work with me on this one." Answer any lingering questions and do any last-minute research.

You might just be greeted with a go-ahead. An interested editor may answer the telephone, extend the offer to write, explain exactly what she's looking for, and note that a contract will follow. If your editor gives you a verbal go-ahead, but no contract, it's to your advantage to confirm the details in an e-mail or a brief letter. This shows professionalism, clarifies any misconceptions, and shows great initiative on your part. Be sure to include the working title, specifics you discussed (people to interview, books to mention), the word count and deadline, price you'll be paid, any photography or artwork that you're responsible for or may need to request from others (perhaps travel bureaus).

If your editor has assigned the article to you, there should also be mention of a kill fee, should she deem your article unfit for publication. Especially in tough economic times, when magazines shrink from insufficient advertising, it's important to negotiate a kill fee. Typically it's at least 25 percent of the agreed-upon price for the finished piece, but it is often unavailable for new writers working on spec.

Completing Your Assignment

Follow any instructions your editor has given you, and write according to the publication's style. Check all facts, showing details instead of telling them, citing examples, quoting resources, and including anecdotes whenever possible. When I say show don't tell, I mean don't write "His circumstances were absolutely pathetic" when you could skip the unnecessary adverb and really write a few sentences about those circumstances in vivid detail.

Ask yourself to fill in the blank in the following statement: "If there's one thing I want my readers to gain from this, it's _____." For this book, I've kept as a reminder—they want to make money . . . and fast.

If you feel your article is getting off on a tangent, crafting a related sidebar allows you to keep the main focus about the primary article, but to include auxiliary material that the reader may enjoy or need. Be sure to write to the assigned word count. Twenty words over is no big deal, but two hundred definitely poses a problem.

Aim for clean, error-free copy. Even if guidelines allow for hand-written corrections, always print a fresh copy. Sufficient white space attracts the eye so keep a one-inch margin all around the pages. Don't forget your name, address, and telephone number, in case your manuscript gets separated from your cover letter.

Ideas + Good Writing = Success!

Read outstanding magazines and newspapers to gather ideas for possible publication. Read widely, for if you are to succeed, you'll need money coming in from several publications, not just one or two. Note the structure these articles take, the length, anecdotes, transitional devices, resources tapped into, and the angle taken. Ask yourself: "What made this article work for me?" Also, combine what you've read with the brainstorming I've referred to earlier. You will find ideas.

Soon, you'll write your own material, too. Ask yourself what you could do to improve your piece. Could photographs add to the appeal? Could quotes make it stronger? Would a different angle be more appropriate? Finally, be open to your editor's suggestions, remembering that he or she knows the audience. The editor knows what is a turnoff and what cancels subscriptions.

Studying the Newspaper Market

Newspapers, big or small, remain fertile grounds for establishing good journalistic practices and developing a consistent track record of meeting deadlines. Frankly, there is no better place to ply your craft and enjoy a faster paycheck since most newspapers publish daily or weekly.

Newspapers are everywhere. Some are quite prestigious. When I moved to the Washington, D.C., suburbs, I had to admit the sheer pleasure in reading the *Washington Post* every day because I was inspired by Woodward and Bernstein cracking the Watergate case. The *Post,* as we call it locally, is one of the nation's finest newspapers. But writers don't start at these havens of talent.

Aim for a community newspaper, a regional parenting publication, a specialty newspaper serving the arts, business, or minority community. While plying your craft, editors get to know your abilities, and you get to determine any areas of specialization you might enjoy. This is where *beat reporting* offers you the chance to cover one area, such as the county court circuit, business, lifestyle, sports, culinary pages, or health. These are all "beats," and each one has a different writer. Reporters might specialize because they offer considerable background. A college minor in one of these subjects may give you the edge. The experience covering any subject—day in, day out—will also hone your reportorial skills like none other.

Writing reviews of art exhibits, concerts, dance performances, poetry readings, restaurants, symphonies, lectures, theater, television, musicals, books, or CDs could also give you your first newspaper opportunities. Imagine getting paid to read your favorite novelist's recent release.

If money motivates, ask about the pay structure. At some papers, the only remuneration the book reviewer receives is a free book. Careful study will also show you whether writers are identified as freelancers or staff writers. If you have educational or real-life experience in the subject matter, let your prospective editor know this. Write sample reviews to prove that you're up to the task.

Find items worth reviewing in your daily paper, especially the Sunday sections that have more listings. Stay in close contact with bookstores, publicists, writer's groups, universities, lecture sponsors, concert promoters, and PR personnel. Always witness the entire work, and have a breadth of knowledge of related material and artists to provide valid comparison.

Sometimes reviewers go over the work first as a novice, then return to search out details and ask critical questions (for instance, why is this concert worthy of a listener's time and money?). This isn't always possible if you are reviewing a limited-engagement performance, but if you're the local dining critic, even the chef can have an off night.

Increase your opportunities by keeping in touch with those who can invite you to sneak previews and send you recent releases. Knowing that a museum exhibit is coming to town or that an author plans a stop on his six-city tour in your town helps you to convince your editor, ahead of time.

Sports reporting is for the knowledgeable and persistent. Competition can be steep, particularly at larger papers, so break in at your community newspaper by offering to cover high school sports, and maybe college teams. Face it, everyone wants to interview the starting lineup on pro teams, and it's the PR job to weed out the awestruck clowns from the serious pack of reporters. A team's media guide will no doubt be of great help and assist you in generating stories. Be flexible because every team operates differently. What might be the perfect time to interview one player may be the worst for another because it's during warm-ups. When writing, use statistics with caution. Carefully chosen and peppered throughout your story, they lend authority; overused and your piece suddenly reads like a math-class word problem.

Quick publishing also occurs on the *op/ed page,* where opinions and editorials appear. Most publications won't pay for letters to the editor, but columns often run that offer varying viewpoints and current analysis from guest writers, particularly those whose opinions resonate and ring with shock, anger, or joy. Here is your chance to air a pet peeve or share some much-learned wisdom; just be certain that you don't appear too scholarly or that your writing isn't an exercise in destroying the opposing viewpoint. Focus your efforts on issues that have public appeal and broad support (or lack of it). Read widely and listen to talk radio and watch television. Telling is easy, but showing is more challenging. Illustrate your points with anecdotes, statistics, and quotations that paint word pictures.

Stringers are often used by national newspapers in outlying areas of the country, and by metropolitan papers in outlying counties. It's frequently less expensive to use a reporter for the occasional story than to hire someone to cover the area full-time. Imagine the prestige of being a stringer for a top newspaper or even news magazine. Even if much of what you write never sees print (as sometimes happens at the last minute), you're cultivating ideas, running these past editors, getting feedback, and plying your craft. Ask the bureau chief or editor if you could become a correspondent in your area. If you know of a particular event or personality making news in your area, jump on the chance to get your story in print. Contact your editor in advance to land assignments, and expect to work hard and fast.

If you've got the staying power to *become a columnist,* with ideas at the ready and the persistence to see a column through those less-than-thought-provoking moments, approach editors with the idea. If you have expertise, it could be an easy sell, especially for a local paper with a niche to fill. Prerequisite qualifications are a vivid imagination, plenty of tenacity, sound judgment, and the ability to keep copy fresh and lively. I once wrote a column for the *Pittsburgh Business Times* on balancing work and family. I had met the editor at a public-speaking engagement, and she remembered my book *Working at Home While the Kids Are There, Too.* When the paper's format changed, she sought columnists and thought of me first, but I still wrote several sample columns to show how I'd approach the concept.

Many writers agree that peppering readers with anecdotes from your personal life helps to make points, shows you're "one of them," and maintains column readership. People learn vicariously through your insights and informed commentary. They are interested in real people, not theory and concepts. Keep your copy conversational, clear, and concise. The more you write, the greater your style develops.

If your column has legs (that is, wide reader appeal), you might *syndicate your work.* It's a writer's dream though a tough sell. Most papers already get wire service feeds, so your material must be a cut above, assuming there is a budget for outside work. Someone at your publication may approach a syndicate for you. Otherwise, make contact yourself. *Writer's Market, The Writer's Handbook, Literary Market Place,* and *Editor & Publisher Syndicate Directory* list these. Syndication companies act as agents on your behalf, packaging your columns, shipping them off to their customers, and sending you your half of the 50-50 split on fees. One column sale in itself doesn't amount to much, but if dozens of papers carry your column, the money adds up.

Comparing Magazines and Newspapers: Different but Alike

A feature is a feature, right? Not necessarily. Both newspapers and magazines are based on solid reporting principles. Yes, the lead's purpose in both is to grab the reader's attention and give that nut graph information. Magazine leads might be longer because newspapers rarely run articles that are several thousand words long. When they do, they're generally written in a series of investigative reports, which are invariably staff written. Newspaper writers have mastered the short, punchy prose that fits into specified column inches. Truly, the story length dictates the size of the lead in either format.

Newspapers pride themselves on their objectivity, incorporating a minimum of opinion that is clearly labeled as such when it does appear. Examples are Dave Barry's work, an advice column, or the editorial page, which are plainly someone's opinion, not the news.

Magazines often take a stance, such as an airline magazine wanting to lure frequent travelers to book their next ticket for one of the destinations featured within the airline magazine's pages. You won't find a cover blurb promising "Top-Ten Crime Capitals to Avoid." What if there *is* crime? Must you check your integrity at the keyboard? Certainly not, but I've found that there is usually some way to couch negative information without disappointing editors.

Newspapers go to great lengths to localize a national story much like most media outlets (including broadcast stations) do today. Magazines, on the other hand, demand the national scope. In fact, a frequent mistake of beginning writers is to localize too much, forgetting to be geographically diverse whether it's a travel piece or a health-related feature quoting only the local pediatrician.

Magazines have long lead times with deadlines that are sometimes months from assignment. Regardless, prolific work habits equal profit. Take six months pondering each assignment, and your success rate (not to mention income) may plummet.

Moreover, both magazines and newspapers feature a wide range of article possibilities from profiles of the famous and ordinary to items that force thought and share information or personal experience. Each runs how-to features, travel items, fillers, humor, and much more.

There is no harm in querying newspaper editors, but don't expect them to use your SASE, or even postcard. The pace in any editorial office is hectic, but at newspapers facing daily deadlines, it's even worse. The best way to approach an editor is still through a well-crafted letter with appropriate clippings sent along as proof that you can write. Then, a few days later, introduce yourself by telephone. Remind the editor of the letter. If there are no opportunities, ask whether you can check back in a reasonable time period. Use the conversation to guide you, but typically, this will be a few weeks to a few months. Try not to call during deadlines (evening for a morning paper; morning for afternoon). If you don't know when the paper publishes, you've got some homework to do before pitching any idea.

Giving Your Article an Afterlife

Think about the waste of energy, time, and talent whenever a writer finished with one assignment quickly files the folders. There is gold in those notes, I'm telling you. Go spin it. Again and again.

When Fred Rogers celebrated an anniversary on public television, I produced a Q&A piece for an airline magazine, a profile of *Mr. Rogers' Neighborhood* for a parenting paper, and quotes in three different features, not to mention a theme-park filler. I received a finder's fee for an idea presented to *USA Weekend* and made contacts that have been helpful to this day. Even when your hunches don't pay off in published work, recycling can advance you.

I've turned my unfortunate onset of heel pain into at least three published accounts, and I've parlayed knowledge of my native Pittsburgh to numerous editors, hopefully erasing images of sooty smoke that is *not* rising over the modern skyscrapers.

Writers should hold on to all reprint and mail-order rights to previously published work. In an era of "rights grabbing," this may be a tall order. Selling reprint rights is sometimes the same idea as self-syndicating, such as getting multiple arts newspapers, city papers, or

Trade Journals and Other Types of Magazines

Professional journals (known as trade magazines or "the trades") target a more narrow audience, but they are a viable playing field for freelancers. While they may not pay as well as their consumer counterparts, editors are often more accessible and willing to assign regular work. Trade editors respond faster because being less known, they have smaller slush piles. On the positive side, this means more work and quicker cash; on the negative side, they aren't as well known. Find trade magazines in *Writer's Market, Encyclopedia of Associations*, and *Bacon's Publicity Checker*, which can all be found at libraries. Once you've selected a few, pitch articles on successful businesspeople, proven business strategies, emerging trends, and management topics, until your editor begins assigning editorial that was generated in-house. Realize that the reader's specific interest equates to more knowledge so you must write at a level that assumes prior knowledge of the topic.

Other places to look for publications include motor clubs, municipalities, major universities and colleges, alumni magazines, special interest groups, even regional presses publishing smaller magazines. If you're like most writers, you won't need to seek new publications, for they almost find you. You can always spot the writer, with an armload of literature, pamphlets, and freebie publications.

parenting newspapers in different cities to run the same piece. One rule of thumb: Never overlap coverage areas. For instance, don't send to both Fort Lauderdale and Miami newspapers.

If nothing more, publishers can't copy your ideas. Recycle and reinvent your research, if not your published work. Repackage those rejections. I've successfully used rejected material, sometimes with only minor revisions, for a new set of readers with another focus. Always write with extension value in mind.

Starting-Out Steps

Ideas are everything in this competitive business of article writing, but if you don't properly present your ideas to magazine and newspaper editors, respectively, they will never see print. When starting out, you should:

- Be certain to read the publications you are pitching to, studying what the editor and ultimately readers require. Conceive your ideas with a service orientation to ensure take-away value.

- Use annually updated writing directories as well as the writing magazines when searching for guidelines and new markets. Don't overlook trade journals in your search.

- Craft queries that not only grab the editor's attention but, in a nutshell, answer: Why the topic, why you, why now, and how. Master the art of selecting and photocopying appropriate clips.

- For even quicker cash, write for a metropolitan newspaper to hone your journalistic skills and learn to meet deadlines. Don't query, but present your background and clips via the mail and by telephone follow-through.

- Reslant and resell articles in booklet form, as reprints, or use the research in multiple projects.

Note

1. Thomas Clark, *Queries & Submissions* (Cincinnati, Ohio: Writer's Digest, 1995), pp. 54–55.

CHAPTER 7

Photojournalism

TRAVEL WRITING AND PHOTOGRAPHY GO HAND IN HAND. THIS CHAPTER tries to strike a balance between the industrious writer eager to make yet another sale and the working professional (writer, PR pro, or some other) needing to supplement text with just the right camera shot to accompany business-related projects. These might include a range of collateral material including annual reports, newsletters, brochures, or perhaps even Web site development.

If you think anyone can chronicle a cruise vacation or incite reluctant travelers to part with hard-earned dollars for some sunny spot, you're kidding yourself. Travel writing is more than simply enjoying the sights and describing them in vivid detail.

Making Money Through Travel Writing

Study travel trends and what readers demand. So what if you love cruises. Maybe other people don't share your love of the high seas and deem cruising to be too expensive. Trends can really guide us in selecting appropriate travel topics, in terms of both destinations and support pieces. Ecotourism, bike trips across country (or fitness walking tours), and people's anxiety over flying in light of terrorism are all societal trends. So are economic concerns.

Think fun and frivolous in conceiving travel topics. Tap into a hidden fascination. Take the classic movie *Gone with the Wind,* for example.

Building a query around the South, the Civil War, or even a country inn called Tara are three possibilities from one nugget. Travel is generally about having fun.

Plenty of travelers have what I call Ritz-Carlton curiosity—a desire to vicariously stay someplace grand, and maybe even luck into an opportunity to do so. I've had the pleasure of staying at some very upscale resorts—places like Caneel Bay in St. John and Nemacolin Woodlands, in a little town south of Pittsburgh, Pennsylvania. Like those who read *People* magazine, plenty are impressed knowing that celebrities visit Caneel Bay, or that many presidents have flown to Nemacolin on helicopter Marine One. Their curiosity and desire don't erase their budget constraints. So if you learn of midweek or off-season specials, build an article around that concept. Help readers figure out how to travel the way they'd like to. While you're at it, incite them with other reasons to visit. Caneel Bay sits smack in the middle of the U.S. Virgin Islands National Park while visitors to Nemacolin can easily tour Frank Lloyd Wright's Fallingwater, an architectural masterpiece minutes away.

Think seasonal, for sure, in this business. Many editors save sunny locales for winter publication when just reading about sandy beaches could banish thoughts of snow and cold, even for a few brief moments. If you know that the Olympics or the Super Bowl is going to be held in Los Angeles, this gives the editor more reason to feature that city because there is guaranteed interest in the destination. Thus, think news hook.

Finally, I've also learned to think creatively. If people temporarily refrain from airline travel, what vacations can they take? If travel is down in general, who must travel? Myrtle Beach and Williamsburg are two places many families drive to, regardless, and business travelers don't have the option of fear so why not make their stays fun. Boost your chances of an acceptance by focusing on top conference cities, what to see while in town, where to eat, and what to buy for friends and family back home.

Who Buys Travel Articles?

While you might think that your best markets are the travel magazines themselves, look at that newsstand again. Special interest publications that serve families, senior citizens, sports enthusiasts, and even avid cooks are all potential markets. Don't forget the RV enthusiast, the engaged couple planning a honeymoon, or the business traveler grabbing that in-flight magazine from the seat pocket.

The Sunday travel sections of large daily newspapers present good opportunities, but I must also warn you that sometimes budgets are lean and wire copy prevails. Still, these are worth a shot with the right idea. You might not think that your local paper has any interest in a feature on the latest theme park to open across the country, and you're probably right. But that paper might well publish the seasonal tours that the historic house in the next town offers from Thanksgiving through New Year's Day as well as the park's outdoor light display.

Travel newsletters cater to diehard travelers wanting to know what makes a trip worthy of their time and money. Regional magazines often feature weekend getaways, particularly in our fast-paced culture where some people never take a complete week away from work.

If you love writing about travel, broaden your income by writing marketing brochure copy or by handling public relations responsibilities for travel and hospitality clients. You'd be writing about the same topics, only on the client side (not as a media representative).

Travelogues also bring in extra cash if you're comfortable speaking before a group and can offer excellent photography. If you have extensive knowledge of one locale, guidebooks could earn you even more money. Many of these publishers offer you a work-for-hire contract. I've done two such jobs in my career and had fun doing both. In one instance, researching a regional guide to Pittsburgh gave me a credential to edit portions of a larger Pennsylvania project for Compass American Guides.

Do You Need to Travel?

This might seem a strange question, but the best answer is yes. Nothing replaces that ability to absorb details and relate firsthand impressions as opposed to the PR spin of guidebooks and press kits. My second answer is: not always, because you can hone the skills of a travel reporter by writing about life on the periphery of wherever you are—that is, museum exhibits, famous homes, parks, trails, and seasonal attractions.

When I researched *The Insiders' Guide to Pittsburgh,* I found a slew of holiday attractions including candlelight tours, special concerts, and train shows. I took the opportunity to visit many of these, and I didn't have to veer far from home.

You may be afraid to travel because of your own budget constraints; I'll tackle that momentarily. Rest assured, there are ways to make travel and research affordable.

Types of Travel Articles

Travel destination pieces provide reliable information while arousing the reader's interest at the same time. Sometimes these tout heavy tourist draws such as Walt Disney World or Washington, D.C., during school breaks.

Special interest travel articles rely on a news peg or some other tie-in that gives an editor a reason for running it, such as the food and wine extravaganza in Aspen each year, or a new exhibit that might draw newcomers to town. Other pegs could be shopping, sports, or food.

The *round-up travel pieces* offer readers many alternatives. This works well for a mass audience scattered all over the country. Magazine editors especially like recommending parks and accommodations from various regions so that any one reader will have reason to enjoy the article.

Next comes the *adventure article.* It's true that good travel writers do best with their own sense of adventure, but here I'm referring more to an adventure for the reader. This could be a scenic drive along a historic or well-known highway, a bike ride through New England, or a hike up Mt. Everest.

Humorous or *personal accounts* comprise another type of travel article. Here, travelers enjoy blending in with the local residents, in organized programs like "Meet the People" or merely on their own. Of course, sharing your own account of a vacation can spark laughter, yet another approach.

Traits of the Travel Writer

In addition to an adventurous spirit, the writer requires enormous energy. Most people go away to kick back, relax, and read a book, but the travel writer always wants to do more than time allows, seeing everything, taking notes, and asking myriad questions. While most families stock up on travel brochures before their trip, the travel writer comes back with a suitcase full of maps, restaurant menus, freebie newspapers, guidebooks, you name it! Every scrap of information, it may seem, is fodder for a sidebar, statistic, or future article.

Organization is paramount. Don't miss the sidebar on what to pack for a trip. Organization means knowing what your story requires and what you're capable of cramming into a few short days. Don't waste time while away on items (facts, statistics) that you could obtain via the Internet.

Travel writing takes self-confidence to ask questions that others ordinarily wouldn't, and patience to wait around for the perfect photograph. That is why turning family vacations into salable travel articles isn't as easy as people assume. However, many writers start out writing from such trips, broadening their horizons as they gain experience.

The travel writer becomes a connoisseur of details, jotting notes in his or her journal that will trigger a flashback later. Journaling becomes a valued tool, according to veteran travel writers. If your goal is to paint word pictures and a panorama of the place you're visiting, you need to describe things using all of your senses. What does the floor tile in the restaurant look like? What is hanging on the walls? I've been to restaurant restrooms that feature individual newspapers on the back of stalls or pipe in Italian music. Such details make the experience memorable.

Landing Assignments

Travel writers submit a story on spec or query with ideas. As we learned in the previous chapter, querying cuts out unnecessary work and leads to a better reputation among editors.

But when you query, don't merely offer to write a 1,200-word feature on Florida, because your editor will likely write this off as "just another Florida query." What's your angle? Why would readers like your article? Why is it timely? Whom will you interview? What can your readers expect to do or see that they haven't done somewhere else?

Good travel writing requires action, like any form of nonfiction writing really. Therefore, your query should maintain the momentum your editor will require just to sit and read your idea. Research what the editor has recently run, what the editorial calendar calls for, and which advertisers support the publication.

Like other nonfiction articles, once you've established a personal rapport with an editor, you might be able to dispense with the formal query. By now, you might pick up the phone to mention that you'll be attending a wedding seven states away, and by the way, it's only a short drive to the Grand Canyon. Would she be interested in a feature, a sidebar for a piece already in progress, or a filler?

Joining organizations like the Society of American Travel Writers helps if you attend meetings, avail yourself of the advice of other members, and proactively seek opportunities to meet those who might invite you to see their new hotel, exhibit, or city renaissance.

Affording Travel on Your Own Lean Budget

Since I already encouraged you to travel for firsthand research, now I'll explain how to afford such a journey. True, most writers cannot underwrite all the expenses of an extensive research trip. I've found there are few perks to the writing world, but one of them is complimentary or discounted travel.

Hotels, cruise lines, convention and visitor's bureaus, and the PR agencies that represent them often sponsor complimentary journeys for writers to gain publicity.

If you're traveling on your own or with your family, it's wise to plan ahead. Contact the visitor's bureau to alert them that you're a writer conducting research, tell them the article has been assigned or whether you're traveling with good hopes of submitting pieces upon speculation, and ask what policies they have for helping journalists like you. Here is where that self-confidence I mentioned comes into play. Ask, or you shall not receive.

Go straight to the PR person for a hotel, resort, cruise line, or tourist board. Sometimes, these individuals tell you to talk with their public relations account executive at a PR firm. Other times, you'll find that the owner or the property manager handles these requests. It's the PR person's job to facilitate research, at the very least by giving you printed or verbal information, and sometimes by rolling out the red carpet to book your arrangements. He or she might offer a free room for the night (generally two nights is reasonable; consider yourself lucky to get more), or agree to lower the rate for journalists. In fact, some publishers insist on a press rate and frown upon accepting anything free. Be reasonable, and don't make too many demands. Asking for assistance with a hotel shuttle is one thing, but demanding a limousine is quite another. Since they covet your favorable impression, you'll probably be given a great room, prime cabin location on a cruise, or something else that nicely surprises you.

It's doubtful that you'll receive complimentary airfare unless you are journeying with an organized press group. Airlines have always been tight with the tickets, but in today's economic climate, even more so. Such a request is probably unreasonable unless you can truly justify the expense on their end. Most airlines will at least help you obtain the lowest-priced airfare for a particular route.

Ask also for complimentary admission to theaters, parks, museums, and other establishments. PR coordinators at these facilities will understand your needs and go out of their way to help you. Write to them, send clips, and introduce yourself. Sometimes, they'll even send you a press pass that is good throughout a specified period (say a calendar year).

When making plans, it's advisable to have your editor write a generic assignment letter, asking people for their assistance with your research. Send this along with your letters. Also, know your magazine's circulation and your article's approximate publication date. If you're covering the cost of the trip yourself, check to see whether you can file an expense report. If so, keep careful receipts and keep expenses to a minimum. Your editor will appreciate your concern for the publication's budget.

Organized Press Trips

I still look back fondly on the ten years I wrote for *Elegant Bride* covering honeymoon hideaways, Caribbean islands, cruises, and Mexican beaches. The editor who hired me to freelance made many opportunities possible, including many press trips.

What is a press trip? Similar to the "fam" or familiarization trips travel agents take, a press trip means traveling with a group of writers, accompanied by a media representative and perhaps several hosts.

Government tourist boards, PR firms, and hotel properties see you as their link to better coverage.

Accept one of these trips, and someone representing the client will call you with all the details and send your airline tickets, press kits, and possibly packing information. If you still have questions, ask what the trip entails. Unfortunately, I've been on Caribbean press trips with writers who couldn't tolerate sun exposure or fussed about sharing a luxurious villa. I often exchanged knowing glances with the frustrated account executive left to explain to the hosting boat captain why one writer isn't joining the group. PR people put their necks out for you, requesting many of these perks. Rest assured, you're usually wined, dined, and given your own accommodations, but you will be traveling with a group, and sometimes you must tolerate the needs of other writers just as they will be patient with yours. If the writer for a travel trade publication needs to see a dozen different rooms of various price categories, so be it. For your assignment, it might not even matter.

A good letter from the account exec or host outlines what is and isn't complimentary. Some meals, taxi fares, beverages, minibars, room service charges, and tipping are your expenses. But, as glamorous, easy, and inexpensive as these trips might seem, they are indeed work. They aren't free vacations. Friends used to tease me about these trips, assuming I was lying in the sun much like the tourists I write for. They didn't factor in the three flights (including some bouncy small aircraft), the ferry boat or seaplane (talk about bouncy) that didn't have room for everyone's luggage, the jam-packed itinerary that took me from one coast to the other, or the threat of Montezuma's revenge. There are downsides to everything including this, though the seasoned writer learns to appreciate the account executive's role and to be a flexible sport about everything.

I've been on great press trips as well as terrible ones. Most hosts are extremely accommodating. On my visit to Peter Island, I warmly remember the general manager rising at an obnoxious hour to join me for coffee, say good-bye, and see that I left without a hitch. The account exec for another trip pulled me aside and personally thanked me for doing without a piece of luggage that wouldn't fit on that seaplane and for putting up with one of our fussy comrades. Account execs are trying to please many people, especially their bosses and clients, not to mention the group they've assembled to travel as a pack. They soon come to remember the high-maintenance types, who will be waiting years for another invite. Having said that, I remember a four-day mad dash all over Acapulco that was led by a rather angry young man who ignored requests by some of us to research certain aspects of our stories. He cemented a negative impression when his job was to do just the opposite.

That trip taught me to specify any special needs ahead of time. Now, when I receive that first phone call I say, "I'd really appreciate a few hours to explore my reader's interests, but I don't want to inconvenience the group. Do you think that will be a problem?" By asserting my needs like this, I've found that I can get a lot more accomplished.

As account executives have told me, finding writers to take press trips is never a problem, but finding the right group of writers often is. When you accept the invitation, you are indirectly agreeing to attend dinners and meet with tourist board officials and hotel managers. Think of it as your price for these perks. Expect this on most press trips, but the better itineraries build in a balance of mandatory meetings with individual exploration.

What else is expected of you? Namely, flexibility, a sense of humor, showing up at the events, proper attire, professionalism, and sensible packing (you may be schlepping that luggage). I've seen writers show off and drink too much. One even stashed a native woman in his room and brought her along for a free meal! And while no one expects the finest resort wear from Bloomingdales, you should dress neatly, in deference to some planned events where government officials and dignitaries might be present. Remember that you're representing your publication. Word of poor behavior can always get back to your editor who will *not* be impressed.

The Sponsored Travel Debate

So travel writing sounds great so far, and I hear you saying that a few meals and cab fares won't break the bank. However, some newspapers and magazines won't accept sponsored travel. They view it as a conflict of interest; afraid you'll feel bought and render a tainted account of your travels. I've always thought that it's the individual writer's integrity that matters most, not who paid the bill. A sponsored trip or a complimentary admission isn't accepted in exchange for a rave review. It's accepted as part of a writer's research. I understand that my job as

Packing for a Press Trip

Getting ready for any trip is a challenge; but add the business element, and you might leave without a few necessary items. Here is a handy list to help you pack your bags so that you don't forget the following:

- Airline tickets
- Passport, driver's license, birth certificate, or other required identification
- Credit cards, traveler's checks, airline miles/frequent traveler card, some cash (especially for tips)
- Carry-on bag with reading material, plenty of business cards, notebook, camera equipment, change of clothing and toiletries (anything you'd need if luggage got lost a day, such as a bathing suit)
- Office travel kit (though remove scissors and other items scrutinized if in carry-on)
- Film (it's more expensive abroad) and Ziploc bags for hand film inspection
- Large handbag for ladies or backpack to conceal or carry items (like cameras) when traveling
- Medications to combat stomach or intestinal ailments, sea sickness patches
- Ordinary medications and vitamins (properly labeled in original containers)
- Proper footwear (with adequate arch support)
- Sunscreen, hat, jacket, sunglasses (and/or reading glasses)
- Collapsible suitcase for return trip (all that literature you'll collect), fold-up luggage cart
- Handheld tape recorder, tapes, batteries, research
- Appropriate, comfortable clothing (per itinerary and plans)
- Foreign money, phrase book, small alarm clock

a travel writer is to produce favorable copy, but if I spot a serious problem, I will not mislead my readers, regardless of who paid for the trip.

Just know that this debate exists because it could influence your sales opportunities. If you want to sell to a publication with policies against sponsored travel, negotiate a press rate if that is acceptable or ask if the publication can pick up your expenses. Barring these solutions, write the expenses off your business income, but consult your tax adviser first.

When Traveling

Always read over your itinerary ahead of time and know something about the destination, so as not to act like a "nervous Nellie" on her first bus tour. Be able to cite a few facts about your magazine (such as circulation) if asked, and keep track of receipts or note incidental expenses. Remember, not too many rum punches either, and always carry your notebook and camera! I'm kidding, but half serious here. There is no such thing as a vacation for a freelancer who seeks the next article placement.

Don't be afraid to ask questions. Talk with other visitors you may encounter while shopping, eating, or waiting around the hotel lobby. Pick up literature whenever it's available. Don't be shy.

Of course, travel safely. Don't venture into areas you know you shouldn't. Drink and eat in moderation, especially if you're not used to the cuisine or the water. And try as best you can to develop the spirit of mañana, when necessary. In many areas outside the United States, life moves at a much slower pace. Do as the natives do and you won't risk being labeled the fussy American.

Above all, allow yourself to experience the destination you've come to discover. Try the native dishes; sink your toes into the sand; shop where the locals do to absorb the ambiance. Sending a hand-written thank-you note to the primary host will also set you apart as being first-class. Follow with any clips and alert the hosts to your publication date. After all, they made your research possible.

Writing Travel Articles

Most travel pieces open with a strong first paragraph, some local history, or hints of the destination's significance, followed by the body copy stepping a reader through actual sights, sounds, flavors, and other pertinent information. If the reader dials the travel agent, you know you've done your job well.

Write according to your editor's guidelines. That means sticking to the established word count and including any information and requested interviews. Double-check all facts and statistics.

In Chapter 6, I discussed the idea of showing, not telling in your prose. Take the reader with you, using action verbs that put him or her in your shoes, careening down the last dip of that roller coaster, skipping along the waves in the catamaran, or drowning yourself in the sun's rays. Leave out hackneyed expressions and popular clichés—watch those similes and metaphors.

Steer readers away from disappointing experiences. If an incident was so bad it was laughable, laugh with it. Putting unfortunate incidents into a humorous light gets your point across without being blatantly offensive. Some editors prefer to see information such as restaurant and hotel options, airline gate cities, relevant Web sites, money exchange tips, and customs allotments placed in a sidebar. Still other editors require the personal touch added to stories. First-person experiences add dimension to your work and provide far beyond what press kits and brochures can already offer a would-be tourist.

Supplementing Income with Good Photography

Photography can not only supplement your text but also increase your income. Some editors won't even touch a manuscript that is not submitted with photography. Thus, crisp, clear 35-mm slides or newspaper black-and-white photographs often clinch the sale.

Photography adds immediacy to your article package. It conveys an ambiance that sometimes cannot be achieved through words alone. Also, photography provided by the writer saves the editor or art director a great deal of time searching for ways to illustrate the story.

All writers benefit when they think visually. Train yourself to think this way, learning to anticipate a good camera angle or action photograph in the making. Remember, it's all about the action, and here, too, photographs can tell a compelling story. Posed snapshots might be fine for the family album, but they won't cut it with any art director (or editor who screens the material first). If your subject works in an office, catch the person looking over papers or chatting with a colleague. Amateurs point and shoot; professionals carefully frame the shot. Unexpected angles add so much more than eye-level photography.

While family photos strive for the all-inclusive feel, cramming everyone into the edges of the frame, these shots are opposite the photojournalist's inclination. Fill every frame, but with a close-up of one or two people, not two dozen. When you do have several people in a shot, be sure to write down their names, proper spellings, from left to right.

Pay attention to background elements, because you don't want plants or poles growing out of people's heads. Imagine a scene differently by trying a distance shot or close-up, various angles and lighting, as well as horizontal and vertical formats. It's so easy to forget, but if you ever want your work to land on a magazine's cover, you'd better turn the camera slightly for a vertical shot, because horizontals simply won't work.

As for lighting, the sun can be a blessing or a curse if your subject is backlit and lost in shadow. Therefore, the savvy photographer shoots with the sun behind one of his or her shoulders, with the light falling onto the subject. If it's a people-oriented shot, your subject might squint from the glare, so these might be best taken in slightly overcast conditions or with some shade. Provide captions and obtain releases to send with your photographs. *Photographer's Market* tells whether model releases are required. Generally, if a person is directly recognizable or if the person's likeness would be used in advertising, you should obtain a release. Some photojournalists worry with releases only for U.S. citizens, but use your judgment and your publication's guidelines to decide.

With today's ever-advancing airport security measures, it's more important than ever to ask for a hand check of your film and photography equipment, which you should hand carry. Your livelihood depends on your film's condition, and if you run into less-than-patient security personnel, you may need to politely insist on a hand inspection. That's why Ziploc bags can be so handy on your packing list. When purchasing film, remember that slow-speed film is best because it produces tighter-grained transparencies, allowing for better magnification and high-quality reproduction.

One of the best resources I've found to aid writers in supplementing their income this way is *Photography for Writers: Using Photography to Increase Your Writing Income* by Michael Havelin. Enrolling in a noncredit class instructed by a professional photographer is another good bet because you'll learn how to choose equipment and operate it to maximum creative and monetary benefit. When you buy your camera, it's a good idea to purchase a full-size how-to-use book (to supplement the guide that comes with your camera) because it will provide plenty of tips.

Purchasing Camera Equipment

As Havelin indicates in his book, you don't need to buy everything all at once, but dealing with a reputable and local camera dealer will show you the range of cameras available. Choose a store with a favorable return policy, and do your homework before browsing.

Most travel writers prefer a single lens reflex (SLR) camera with interchangeable lenses, but I've known many writers who achieve equivalent sales using automatic 35-mm models. These "idiot cameras" (as they're called by the pros) choose your shutter speed and aperture opening and frame the shot for you. If that is how you must begin, so be it. With time, your talents will improve and you'll advance to the next level of sophistication in photographic equipment.

Consider cameras you can add to with extra equipment. While the basic telephoto lens suited me fine for family vacations, I soon discovered the benefits of a zoom once I began travel writing in earnest. If you take a lot of action shots, an automatic rewinder is a must. If you do a lot of indoor work, purchase fancier flashes. Analyze what you think you'll need, talk with other photojournalists, and seek the advice of trusted dealers. Salespeople might try to charm you with more than you need, but if they understand you are a professional just starting out, they'll stand to gain a lot more by winning your trust. Convince them of this.

Choosing Color vs. Black and White

Remember that editors love color. Provide this, and you might be on to a quicker sale. Having said that, color adds to the cost of publications in most cases.

If you do a significant amount of public relations or newspaper work, there is inherent beauty, or an art, about black-and-white photography. It's actually made a comeback in everything from wedding photography to annual reports and corporate brochures as well as magazine advertising, especially when budgets are leaner.

In black-and-white photographs, objects are reduced to their fundamentals of line and texture. Without the benefit of color to reinforce interest and organize elements, a black-and-white photograph needs exceptional composition; a strong concept; and, of course, talent that some photographers acquire only by practice in this medium. What makes a better halftone than another? Sharp focus, finer grain, the juxtaposition of dark and light tones creating surface detail, highlight and shadow detail, and overall contrast of deep blacks and bright whites with intermediate grays in between. Don't be surprised if your superb skill in color photography doesn't immediately translate into the same success with black-and-white photographs.

Starting-Out Steps

Travel writing and photography may provide an extra source of revenue for articles and your client work. If you produce business newsletters, annual reports, and the like, you'll need to wield a camera, even occasionally. Many times a complete photojournalistic

How to Obtain Stock Photography

On occasion, an editor or client will request photography from another source. For travel articles, you'll find that convention and visitor's bureaus or local tourist boards will be more than helpful, and often their PR firms step up to fulfill your request with just the right set of slides. You might need to simply coordinate the editor's request with the timing of your submission. A few phone calls, faxes, or e-mail messages are usually all this takes. Other times, you may need to search broader. *Photographer's Market* might prove very useful in your search.

Producing Travelogues

One of the old standbys of travel entertainment is the travelogue, which admittedly in this high-tech age might be on the way out in favor of 360-degree screens and IMAX presentations. Still, you might add some additional income by turning those breathtaking slides into a presentation that tells a story. Sell any guidebooks or reprints after your presentation for extra income.

Effective travelogues tell a story with a variety of photographic images, angles, and shots. Some are long range, medium range, and closeup. Every time you change locale, you should incorporate an identifying shot that symbolizes the location. The Eiffel Tower or a French woman holding a baguette tells us we're now in France, as do words on photographed signs.

Organize your best slides on a light box so that you can see each shot in relation to the last and the one ahead of it. Plot out your presentation, and write your notes loosely rather than in a form that you would read. This way you can speak extemporaneously. Jump to Chapter 8 about speeches for more insight here on practicing your commentary that accompanies your photographic work.

When giving your presentation, allow your audience to ponder the scenery before switching scenes too quickly. Let them feast their eyes on each shot for approximately six seconds until changing to another scene. Generally, a 140-slide tray or two 80-slide circular trays should be sufficient for an individual presentation.

package is your ticket to an editor's acceptance. Keep in mind the following tips:

- Learn to think visually because this will help your photos to convey a story as much as text. Plan shots with sale possibilities in mind. Always take more shots than you think you'll need because it's easy to weed out the technical errors and terrible takes.

- Look for a niche in the travel market that is waiting to be filled—from the single crowd to senior citizens. Approach editors with specific angles in mind.

- Venture into unfamiliar territory with your brainstorming of destinations; avoid overdone tourist spots. Also, focus queries on destinations that have sufficient advertising support.

- Seek PR contacts for the destinations you'd like to write about, introduce yourself, and inquire about upcoming press trips.

- Join the Society of American Travel Writers for networking and other benefits.

- Earn additional income by producing travelogues if you are able to combine speaking, photographic, and presentation skills.

CHAPTER 8

Teaching, Speaking, and Specialized Jobs

WRITING IS SUCH AN ISOLATED ENDEAVOR THAT GETTING OUT AMONG other writers, including those who wish to learn from your accomplishments, is healthy. First, it creates a social opportunity, even in distance education mode or online courses. Second, if you really want to learn something well, teach it to another person. Teaching and speaking about your craft will make you a better writer. Third, the writing-related jobs in this chapter can supplement your income. With fees sometimes ranging up to several thousand dollars a day, teaching others to write might actually pay better than sitting behind a keyboard some days.

Why Impart Your Knowledge?

Beyond the benefits I just cited, teaching is an excellent foundation for writing a book because students' questions and observations are fodder for what you must cover. Teaching stretches your knowledge as you answer questions. You become more comfortable in your own accomplishments while learning to promote yourself.

There is also more immediate feedback as well as the camaraderie of fellow writers. Beginners will eagerly seek your instruction, advice, and encouragement. My spirits soared when I received these comments from a former student: "I'm writing to thank you and share some of my successes with you. . . . Since taking your class, I've been working hard at freelance writing, and so far it's paid off. I'm glad to tell you that I've sold FOUR articles, and one slogan to a greeting card company." This student shared how motivated she felt with the new direction her career had taken. That e-mail really made me smile. All of us appreciate feedback. Similarly, another former student thanked me when she landed her first book contract. Some former students have stopped me in stores and elevators telling me how much they learned, how they can now stay home with their children, or how they began essentially a new and fulfilling career. Such comments inspired me to take what was always a successful classroom model and teach it via distance learning.

Teaching and public speaking are not get-rich-quick means of remuneration. However, if you conduct seminars for corporations with a training budget, the larger the company, the more lucrative you may find it. Plus, teaching provides you with a steady paycheck while you're working on projects that might not pay for months. In that sense, it *is* quick cash. The pay ranges vary from an hourly rate to a set fee for adjunct classes, an honorarium for a speech, or certainly a salary for a part-time or full-time faculty post. Don't be surprised though if students partake of your manuscript critiquing services and buy your books or articles. Teaching and public speaking are built-in promotion vehicles for writing-related services or products. Active professionals who love what they do and make a living at it make the best instructors for courses and seminars, and the possibilities abound.

Teaching Opportunities

If you want to teach, there is surely an option for you. Whatever course you can create and research, you can propose to colleges and universities, business and trade schools, companies, corporations, public schools, continuing education programs, or professionally run seminars across the country. No two courses are alike, and the necessary credentials depend on the academic level you're teaching. You'll need to know more than your students, enough to field questions and speak from personal experience, but for others, you don't always need to know that much more to be considered an expert in your field. Writer's conferences may tap you for panel presentations and workshops, even if you've only written for a few years.

Colleges and universities rely heavily on advanced degrees and publishing credits to determine whether they'll hire you. While any teaching requires organizational and interpersonal skills, these are paramount in the academic classroom. You'll spend greater blocks of time researching and preparing your lectures, counseling students, and grading their assignments.

Adjunct teaching is a good way to start out if you're somewhat unfamiliar to academe. It's different from the tenure-track teaching positions, and you can often get by with only a master's degree and significant work-related experience. As one prominent faculty member at a journalism school once told me, if they want you bad enough, they may even bend the rules. The pool of available talent changes each semester; so if an adjunct spot appeals to you, persist in contacting department chairpersons, perhaps even quarterly until a spot arises.

Business and trade schools usually require an emphasis on writing letters, memos, reports, and other business correspondence. In fact, businesses themselves may want to bring you in to address a particular deficiency that is widespread among employees. Community colleges or workforce development programs therein coordinate these, sometimes at the employer's offices. Corporate training is probably the most lucrative of all teaching opportunities.

Public schools may need journalism teachers and adult sponsors of the high school yearbook or newspaper where you'll guide students who contemplate careers in journalism. You'll need to have a college degree and several education credits including some student teaching experience and security clearances to work with children. Summer career camps are also an option for extra income.

You might try serving as a writer-in-residence whereby you live in the setting where you teach for typically a week at a time, usually during the summer months at some retreat location. Check with the National Endowment for the Arts and state councils for the arts to learn about these opportunities. Fellow writers and writing magazines can offer hints on where to look as well.

The most popular form of teaching is, by far, adult continuing education. The graying of America and the need for retooling and continuing to update one's skills tell us that these program offerings are here to stay. Conveniently, many are held in the evenings and on weekends because adults have other commitments, namely employment. There's usually no course credit involved, but sometimes students earn continuing education units or certificates. Some freelancers who create popular courses in these divisions branch out into independent seminars, where they have greater control and earn much higher incomes.

Distance education is also becoming quite popular. Born of necessity and technological advances, many students enroll in Web-based training, e-mail correspondence courses, or formal distance-learning programs because it fits their busy lifestyle, geographic location, and sometimes just because they prefer it. Online instructors can often break lessons into more manageable units and make assignments that students complete at their convenience, as they work at an individual pace.

Regardless of the educational option, your challenge is to create an intriguing course description that will excite students to register and participate in your class.

Proposing a Noncredit Course

Since lifelong learning is a definite trend, I'll focus here on how to create a noncredit class. Most teaching follows this same organizational stage. Your course description will be your primary publicity vehicle so take time writing it, including instructional objectives, a general course description, and a detailed curriculum outline. It's important to note your credentials, any ancillary materials the students will be required to purchase, and what equipment or facilities you'll need to instruct the class. I've offered an in-class video and my writing books as the text. I'm not one to lecture from the book, and good thing. This would annoy students who might feel they've wasted time and money. Instead, my books have always been a source of encouragement when our time together ends, for it's easy to be inspired an hour after a workshop, but in two months? If you have handouts that need to be photocopied or collated, plan ahead to get the materials to the department personnel or compile books yourself and charge a separate fee, especially for article reprints.

Most continuing ed programs run workshops spanning a few hours to several sessions held weekly for two to twelve weeks. If your course meets weekly, aim for six or eight weeks rather than ten or twelve, since most adults are willing to make a commitment but prefer a shorter duration.

Tempt your students with a course description they simply can't refuse. You want them to feel that they absolutely *must* sign up or they'll miss something important. Use words such as "how-to . . . you . . . new . . . and proven." Combine these suggestive words with action verbs such as "discover," "earn," or "succeed."

I've called my popular writing class by many names, but in all cases, I deliberately kept the focus on money because my students all sought additional income. If your course meets occupational as opposed to avocational criteria, the college has a better chance of receiving funding and/or getting approval in a future roster. Writing, public relations, desktop publishing, newsletter production, and public-speaking classes have the potential of helping people in new or existing careers.

Write your descriptions with advancement in mind. Don't make lofty promises that students will get rich or change their lives, even though they very well could. Advertise so that potential participants bring a lot of hope and promise with them that first session. Be honest about class content. If there is a lot of hands-on work involved, tell them. If there are prerequisite courses, state these in your description. Tempt students by saying, "Find out the six essential steps to successful article sales." Of course, don't list these six points in your promo copy, but unveil them in your lectures. Any add-on costs (such as books) need to be disclosed in promotional copy, and you may need reminders such as to bring a checkbook for materials or to submit draft copy for critiquing ahead of time.

Courses must attract a minimum number or face cancellation. I've often promoted classes with flyers, posting them at libraries; around campus; or, in the case of the Internet, through e-mail. Your material should be simple, often omitting price so as not to give anyone a reason to dismiss enrollment without careful consideration. Make students ponder and inquire further. Ask editors of suburban papers to list your workshop under the calendar of upcoming events. Perhaps your cable channel runs community announcements free of charge. All of these efforts boost enrollment, and that is what counts, particularly if your program bases your pay upon a percentage of paid attendees.

Every Class Is Unique

Often I'll get an exceptionally good group that bounces ideas off each other, fully participates, and truly sees the value in what I'm teaching. Every so often, however, there is that one student, like the woman who signed up for a public relations class because antiques was cancelled. She balked at the first writing assignment and happily found a home in microwave cooking the next week. Talk about mismatched expectations. Only twice in fifteen years have students complained to coordinators. In each case, mismatched objectives played a part. One student complained that the class wasn't entertaining enough. Well, I've never quite marketed my teaching as a stand-up routine. Another older woman was particularly miffed because after plopping a booklet in front of me to critique, I obviously didn't tell her what she wanted to hear. The course description never implied manuscript criticism, and I was very diplomatic in telling her she had a great idea that required further development.

While disgruntled students concern me, I've come to realize that you cannot please everyone. Some want more writing exercises; others want fewer. One wants the class to be longer while the next desires a more compact curriculum. You can learn from student criticism, however. If evaluations uncover that you didn't answer all questions, encourage students to jot down questions to review at the end. Some instructors build consulting time into their fees (or charge extra afterward) so that for a period of thirty days perhaps, they will critique something sent by students.

Online instruction is much the same, with some groups seeming to gel better than others. Despite an instructor's encouragement to politely critique other students' work, some students either feel they aren't qualified to do so, or else they're so zealous in their criticisms that they alienate their classmates.

Preparing Your Lessons

I format my lectures (even in distance teaching) with notes. I update these periodically, and section off each lecture in my notebook or hard disk, placing copies of handouts, answers to quizzes, and discussion items in that section for any given module. As a reminder to myself, I type at the top of each session what I'll need to bring to the physical classroom, lest I forget something while rushing out the door.

I've also found over the years that students love a syllabus as much as handouts and freebies (writing magazines, bookmarks). If it's an ongoing class, I list minimal homework assignments, which are hopefully some fun, requiring students to read certain chapters in my book or to study newspapers, magazines, card counters, or whatever we're discussing. This works especially well if you offer distance education courses where there isn't any face-to-face contact. Software from Variety Games allows you to make entertaining but educational word searches and crossword puzzles as a diversion for your students. Simply type in class terminology, and it creates the puzzle for you. Then, you can write the definitions or clues for students to complete the puzzle assignment.

Quick phone calls or e-mails prior to the first class might ensure that everyone enrolled shows up for the first session. If the number of attendees determines your pay, be sure to do this.

Making Your Class a Success

Always remember that writing may be a dreaded subject to many, especially in the corporate sector. If you instruct fellow writers, they may share your enthusiasm, but still be dissuaded by unsettling fears. Trial and error will be your best guide. Just as readers require a strong writer's voice when perusing text, students want the instructor's perspective. For that reason, limit outside speakers. If there is a recognized professional you want to bring in, do it for only thirty minutes, certainly not more than an hour. Otherwise, you are seen as less of an authority. Mention other classes that these authorities may teach. Mention their book, but keep control of the classroom setting.

Instructors report that audio and video presentations haven't always gone over too well. I once used *The Elements of Style Video,* but students have reacted much more favorably to a video describing the publishing process with interviews of various professionals in the field. Again, the lesson here: Keep control. Students want you, not someone else.

Students also want to practice. Teaching students to write without giving them the opportunity to do so would be the equivalent of driver's education without ever getting behind the wheel. Students have said practicing in class helped pinpoint strengths and weaknesses—my intention all along. If you're unsure about how much in-class writing to include, just remember the word "workshop" implies work. Let the time limits and course duration guide you. A 70/30 ratio of lecture/work is fair for a classroom model. Distance education, where students often create knowledge for each other, is heavier on independent learning, research, writing, and assignments.

Many authors who teach make their books available either by incorporating them as a text or by simply alerting students to their existence. I'll often keep my books on the table up front and make an order form available if students have further interest. Some have actually walked away from class with signed books to give as gifts. It's fine to cite the book in an example to illustrate a teaching point, but there is a fine line between this approach and blatant sales pitches. You're obviously there to teach first. If your book is the class text, don't repeat what students can read independently.

Setting Up Seminars

The primary advantage of teaching through a school system is that the school takes care of the location, registration, and promotion. But it also takes quite a cut for the services rendered.

If you've developed a successful teaching style and are looking for greater financial windfall, sponsor your own seminar, according to Gordon Burgett, who has offered thousands of seminars and tapes. Of course, with the potential for profit also comes the risk of cancellation and financial loss. When you self-sponsor seminars, you book the hotel, classroom, or public meeting hall. You rent the microphone and other audiovisual equipment. You pay for the direct-mail campaign and promotion. If you end up having to cancel, most of that money is lost.

But if you've found a need waiting to be fulfilled, sponsoring a seminar may be that next step in your teaching career. Focus on a service orientation. Set out to make your seminar participants healthier, wealthier, or wiser, and your idea stands at least a running chance. Your audience will expect a comfortable public meeting place. Contact the local Chamber of Commerce or Convention and Visitor's Bureau to find out the names of appropriate facilities. Schools, churches, and libraries may be able to offer you the space you're looking for, while charging a minimal fee.

Seminars that last an entire day or longer are risky because few people want to commit the time unless they understand the true value. Factor into your decisions the weather and conflicting commitments because any seminars sponsored in November or December are too crowded by holiday activities to draw a sufficient audience. Students may also be reluctant to sit indoors on a bright summer day or travel a distance in bad weather. My pick for successful seminar months would be March through May as well as September and October, when people tend to be more focused on learning after the summer hiatus.

Offering your own seminar creates questions regarding sales tax levied on product sales and whether you need to hire any additional help or offer food. Your state taxing authority can guide you. Consider a fictitious name for your business and make arrangements for credit card sales as well. And, if you do have product sales going on, or if you simply expect a large crowd, have another set of hands to register people and collect money.

Coffee and donuts often wake people up and put smiles on their faces. I'd skip lunch altogether unless you plan a networking experience or need food service to get a lower room rate at some hotels. Food choices always increase costs. You might encourage students to stick together in groups as they purchase their lunches to learn more about each other's goals and experiences, and to build a network of support.

Public-Speaking Opportunities

Teaching and speaking require many of the same skills, only here you might be presenting to aspiring writers in bookstore settings, writer's conferences, community groups, or schools as a guest lecturer. What are people concerned about? Use your knowledge of trends, scour the bestseller lists, and tune into the news and comedy channels to discover a niche. What aspect of your craft are you most knowledgeable about, such as overcoming writer's block, finding motivation or ideas, promotion tactics? Find out what your audience cares about most and build your anecdotes, examples, and word pictures around this.

Watch the best speakers you can find, either in person or by video

Increasing Your Income

If making as much money as possible is your goal, focus on corporate training. Encourage people to sign up fast with a deposit. In your promotions, state that space is limited. Discount early registration if you can. Promote the tax deductibility of your seminar for professionals. In addition, when you register participants, always get their names, phone numbers, and addresses. Keep this information for future mailing lists, book promotions, or teaching opportunities.

Price any job-related workshop that can be billed back to employers slightly higher than those created for seniors or beginning writers. If your goal is to attract consulting clients or sell back-of-the room (BOR) products, then the fee is secondary. Overall, if you keep the benefits of taking your seminar high and the costs to yourself (and your students) low, you'll maximize your profit.

Provide a handout on how participants can reach you following the seminar. You could bill separately for editorial critiquing, even of business correspondence for corporate attendees, but check first with those who hired you. They may want this to be factored into the sessions themselves. Offer follow-up courses or consultation in specialty areas, for instance in technical writing, letter writing, e-mail, and memo correspondence. Ask for a portion of your fee up front for preparation.

Charge a separate materials fee. When I started teaching, self-serve photocopies were half the cost of what they are today. The expenses add up, not to mention the cost of your time preparing materials. Finally, whenever you must travel for corporate training or a conference, insist in your contract that the host pay travel expenses. Likely, you'll not be compensated for your travel time.

Of course, you don't want to price seminars too high, but price them too low and there is no perceived value either. It truly depends on who creates the content. If you do, obviously you need to charge more. Some writing instructors online make approximately one-third of the published course cost to students, but these are instances where there is no course development work, just critiquing assignments and answering questions. Other programs pay a percentage of fees, but if students pay minimally for a seminar, you must work with a lot of students to make those seminars pay off.

or audiotape. Take notes to discover how they successfully connect with the audience, make their presentations enjoyable, and if you're there in person, scour the BOR sales. It's said that people retain roughly 10 percent of a presentation. Thus, BOR sales are necessary and profitable. Many conferences automatically record and sell their seminars on cassettes. That cuts into your BOR profits. When negotiating your speaking fee, charge more up front.

Professionals realize that the first and last thirty seconds of presentations have the most impact. Speak from the heart, and just be yourself. Personal anecdotes work wonders. Discuss your first sale, your biggest mistakes, the strangest publications (or editors) you've worked with (just don't name names!), your most embarrassing or funny experiences, or what made you really angry or happy. The goal is to connect with and move your audience, by opening up or using self-deprecating humor. Whenever you end a point, be sure to maintain eye contact. Remember to instruct and show how your listeners can apply what you're telling them in their lives. If you quote statistics or other people, have the reference in front of you as a visual cue, but don't overquote or you'll look less the expert yourself.

Involve your audience with rhetorical questions that keep them thinking by asking for a show of hands. You might talk about the typical life of a writer, asking everyone to stand, and as you ask, "Has this ever happened to you?" have them sit back down. The technique is another way to keep people in tune with you, and to give them a sense of participation. Any time you offer a Q&A session, be sure to repeat the question for those who didn't hear it, and answer in one or two points. Don't allow one person to dominate the session, and if you're asked something you don't know, promise a reply (ask for a business card with the question scrawled on the back).

You'll want to think visually and carefully employ props that keep your audience's attention. For instance, a psychologist author might have a bag of items families fight over the most, such as a television remote representing control and decision making; a checkbook, to represent spending; a Christmas card, to show how holiday chores are divvied up—you get the idea. Throughout her talk, she reveals one at a time. Tape-record each presentation, and listen later to how you sound. Take notes on improvements to make in your next presentation.

Editing and Proofreading

Wherever you see words in print, there has been a proofreader and/or an editor, steadfastly double-checking spelling and punctuation. For most nonfiction books, an indexer has helped you get through the material without your even realizing it. If you want to build better industry contacts, add to your skill set, and earn extra money, check out these specialized jobs.

Without a proofreader or editor, we readers would be bogged down in the latest annual report or lost as we unwound with a good novel. Not only will you find work in major publishing houses but also at print shops, typesetting firms, magazine and newspaper offices, in-house corporate printing departments, and university presses. If you have specialized knowledge, say of medical terminology or scientific jargon, contact companies and publishers of highly targeted material. While proofreaders concern themselves with the finer points of the printed product, editors concentrate on the acquisition, development, and content of the work. Content editing begins as soon as a project is developed. Copyediting is concerned with line editing facts, figures, grammar, spelling, style, word usage, and punctuation.

You'll need that steady sense of proper spelling, grammatical accuracy, and an aura of nitpickiness to succeed. Typographical errors slip into text so easily. While most companies or publishing houses follow one of the standard stylebooks, others have developed additional house stylebooks to ensure a uniform appearance.

Never proof your own work. We all tend to marry what we write, and when we read it back, we see what we think is there rather than what actually is. Proofreading from a hard copy is much easier on the eyes than proofing from a computer screen.

The freelance editor works closely with publishers and other writers recognizing marketable concepts, and organizing several issues in advance, shepherding assignments, even setting artificial deadlines. They edit content without sacrificing the writer's voice, which makes each project unique. No microediting, in other words. When marking up copy, some experts suggest using a color other than red, for red is often seen as a stop symbol, sometimes making others resist change.

Proofreading usually pays by the hour, but perhaps you can strike a retainer. Ask other freelancers what they charge or inquire with your local printer. Finding work as a proofreader or editor begins with a letter of introduction citing publication experience and specific knowledge. Don't be surprised if you're given a proofreading or editing test.

Literary Market Place (available in most libraries) includes listings of publishers and editorial services open to proofreaders. Sometimes the classified ads are helpful as well as *Publisher's Weekly, Writer's Market,* and *The Writer's Handbook.* In addition, the Editorial Freelancers Association in New York City serves as a clearinghouse for all types of editorial personnel and offers meetings, educational opportunities, publications, and job postings with paid membership.

Reading and evaluating the market potential of novels and nonfiction projects helps you to pocket additional income. However, each person desperate for a critique also wants to know "what's in it for me?" You need to provide an answer of what you can offer that some other experienced writer or editor cannot. Specify how you'd like the work to appear. I learned not to assume that material would come to me double spaced when I was sent handwritten manuscripts.

Never promise a guaranteed sale or polished manuscript in return. Novices hang their hopes on these, but you can only promise to evaluate, point out strengths and weaknesses, suggest solutions, and give encouragement. If you are truly impressed with the caliber of the work, strike a collaboration agreement. Nearly ten years before publication of *The Angry Child,* my coauthor Dr. Tim Murphy asked me to review his book proposal. I believed his idea had great market potential from the start, but it wasn't until years later that the idea struck us to work together at getting it published because of his hectic schedule. How I wish we had collaborated and brought the book out sooner.

Indexing as a Freelance Career

A book without an index is like a library without a database. Indeed, it's frustrating to grab the right reference and never know where to find an entry. A book's index solves this. Short monographs, major texts, and academic journals also require an index, even more so for highly technical or medical data or historical records.

The American Society of Indexers (ASI) has a wealth of information on its Web pages. In most standard publishing contracts, there is an index clause though rarely do authors compile these themselves. Typically a freelance indexer, often working from home, is hired by the publishing house to compile the index, and the publisher, in turn, charges the expense against the author's future earnings. Most use specialized software packages.

Qualifications include excellent language skills, an orderly mind, and a capacity for the intake of many data, plus high clerical aptitude, accuracy, and attention to detail, and business savvy.

Before investing in software, read books and attend a workshop or class at a local college with a library or information science program. These often offer indexing courses, and there are correspondence courses available, according to the ASI, through the U.S. Department of Agriculture.

An indexer receives book page proofs at the same time as the final proofreading. The indexer lists headings, subheadings, and the location of each pertinent reference, often on index cards with one entry per card. After proofreading these against the page proofs, indexers alphabetize the cards, analyze them for any unintended entry duplication, and cross-reference various listings. Because this is one of the final stages before going to press with a project, there often isn't much time so you must work quickly and accurately.

I've often been asked if you couldn't just compile an index similar to a concordance (a list of words/phrases and where they appear) on your own personal computer. Those in the industry say it's about concepts not just words and providing answers to a host of unasked questions. Computers can do this, but they fall short when it comes to understanding and organizing the information. A good software package accomplishes indexing tasks according to rules you specify (such as letter-by-letter or word-by-word alphabetizing or by order of page reference), allows for different type styles and fonts, keeps entries in separate formats so that you can change the arrangement, and comes equipped to provide a wide variety of layout options to meet different publishers' requirements. It will have effective search/replace ability and provide various types of searches including Boolean; offer import, merge, and spell-check capability; and be compatible with whatever computer platform or hardware you use. Essentially, human skill and the best software package you can afford make the difference. In addition, the finished index can be delivered on disk or CD-ROM, via the Internet, in simple text files, or as camera-ready copy

Prior editorial or library experience adds to your credentials when you seek employment as an indexer. To obtain job leads, get yourself listed in *Writer's Market, Books in Print,* and *Literary Market Place.* Freelancers send letters and résumés to publishers, accompanied by a list of indexed projects and often a sample index that may clinch the opportunity.

As an independent contractor, you can set your prices. Most quote by the page or per entry. Different publishers prefer different pricing methods. You should price databases or journals differently from books. Perhaps you'll prefer to quote by the hour, especially when you start out. Certainly, you can't charge the same as an indexer with ten to fifteen years of experience, but you can learn by what other professionals charge and increase over time. Both parties benefit from negotiation. Understand that facing budget constraints, many clients want a predictable price, but fixed bids are riskier for you. Be familiar with the project's complexity before boxing yourself into a bid. Specify the expected number of entries per page or in the whole index ahead of time, and also define what constitutes an entry and how these will be counted. You don't want to end up working at the equivalent rate of a fast-food clerk so learn as much as possible before you proceed.

Starting-Out Steps

Look upon teaching, public speaking, editing, proofreading, and indexing as opportunities to keep the cash flowing into your freelance business. Often these jobs pay far faster than long-term writing projects, and you'll enjoy the perks of camaraderie, networking, and career growth as well. When starting out, you should:

- Research education possibilities via the Internet and by obtaining course listings and curricula from schools and conference/seminar promoters.

- Determine what type of teaching endeavor fits your educational background and interest. Analyze whether you need to improve your credentials for certain types of positions, and make those plans accordingly. Don't forget that lifelong learning is a trend that is here to stay. You can fulfill this niche with classes, seminars, and public speaking.

- Creatively use your teaching to make others aware of your business services for manuscript evaluation, book purchases, or other products/services, but be savvy in your promotions.

- Never underestimate the power and sales potential of public speaking, even if it only enhances your recognition to garner future (and better-paying) assignments. Tape your presentations for sale if you want to dub these onto cassette tapes.

- Seek opportunities for specialized writing-related jobs at publishing companies, print shops, publications, and university presses as well as private corporations and industry. Familiarize yourself with standard proofreading marks, common indexing techniques, and available software.

CHAPTER 9

Business and Technical Writing

MOST WRITERS WHO FREELANCE FULL-TIME HAVE WORKED SUCCESS-fully in some form of business or technical writing, if not in public relations or proposal development. Many writers claim that it is far more lucrative than writing for magazines, newspapers, or other media. After reading this chapter, you can determine whether there is a fit for your talents and educational background.

Without effective communication, the business world would cease to attract new clients, customers, and government support. In addition, without public relations and writing support, the media would often report only half the story. In a good economy, there are plentiful staff positions to choose from; in a weaker economy where outsourcing takes place, the freelancer can provide services no longer fulfilled by staff.

When writing for business or technical clients, you're free to take on as many projects as you can manage, often without a byline. A large amount of ghostwriting occurs in the business world, and the person's name appearing by your carefully crafted words might actually belong to your boss. Thus, be prepared for work-for-hire agreements and sometimes little prestige.

On the plus side, there is plenty of interpersonal contact, such as client meetings, as you learn your subject and review project drafts. Whereas you may wait six months for acceptance or payment at a major magazine, you'll often quickly know the status of your work, sometimes within the same day of delivery. Except for the occasional slow-paying client, you'll receive prompt payment for the most part. The best case is that you establish a retainer agreement with one or more clients for steady income.

In this arena, you might write commercial reports for insurance companies, news releases for the media, annual reports for stockholders, corporate histories, financial presentations, collateral materials and business manuals, executive speeches, feature articles for executives, technical literature, video scripts, or work produced for creative agencies. You might also generate proposals for new business. If you specialize in medical or health-care writing, you might research and write reports for several health-care-related clients.

Where to Find Business and Technical Writing Jobs

You'll find many of these projects at small-, medium-, and large-size businesses. Contact department heads in specific areas. Write to them, citing examples of your work. Set up an appointment to show your portfolio. Ascertain the company's writing needs, and seek ways to match them with your skills. If you cannot obtain a face-to-face meeting, mail photocopies of your best examples.

Creative agencies, especially those that do not place large amounts of media advertising, concentrate more heavily on producing collateral materials and providing PR services for their clients. These agencies may also be more receptive to freelance talent. And if you previously worked for a business or industry, nonprofit organizations, schools, libraries, government agencies, hotels or parks, knowing the inside track and who the decision makers are may be your ticket to additional freelancing in public relations. Capitalize on your contacts.

Sometimes specialization pays off. Pharmaceutical or health-care information technology companies, provider organizations, insurance companies, associations, public policy research companies, or even the health-care divisions of law offices will pay for the services and knowledge of a medical or health-care writer. Those writers report that their substantive knowledge of medical and science issues justifies their charging a higher rate. Some can easily clear six-figure incomes, even after expenses. If you have such a background, look to these kinds of organizations. As with many other forms of business or technical writing, you might find that your first client is a former employer. One satisfied client opens the door to many others.

Working with a Variety of Clients

You are only half of the consultant/client relationship, and if you're used to doing things your way—from all those months of working solo—adapting to the business culture might be a culture shock.

Conduct your business as if it were your company, but resist marrying each project when you're called upon to revise or even start completely fresh. While there is truth to the saying "the client's always right," there have been times clients wanted me to proceed in ways I knew were counterproductive, like going to print with incorrect information just to get the job completed. When this happened, I stood my ground.

It's great when we can choose our clients, but often we must take whatever work is available. There will always be clients you merely tolerate. Depending on your circumstances, that is where you set not only professional but personal standards. When my oldest son was in part-time child care, I could easily attend meetings, factoring in the travel time. That all changed when my second son was born severely premature. I only took on family-friendly clients whose projects could be done 100 percent from home. That limited my opportunities for a few years, but for the right reasons. You'll make your own choices based on earning capacity, convenience, and career building. Each client you take on is a learning opportunity, a chance to expand your portfolio, and you never know where that might lead.

Public Relations Work and Tasks

Public relations is not advertising because you don't pay for the time or space involved. Clients pay a staff person, an established PR agency, or a freelancer/consultant like you to earn them coverage through timely, professional, and informative exchanges. But herein lies the problem. Because of its intangible nature, the field of public relations continues to be a hard sell. Decision makers can track advertising very easily, seeing the payoff. Public relations efforts simply aren't that easy to track.

You'll never know the exact number of people who read the notice in the paper or who heard the teaser on air. You may never know how many recipients read your newsletter. If you can sell PR's importance to prospective clients, however, your income potential has no limit.

Specific PR tasks such as annual reports and news releases will be discussed briefly, but sometimes you're called upon to develop a campaign and create an image for a client. You'll need to find out a great deal of background about the organization, its key players, current goals and objectives, as well as how others perceive the organization. If there is a critical image problem you're trying to overcome for the company, how will you bring about that change between what is and what could be?

Once you know your objectives, you can solicit the opinions of others within your client's organization. Many nonprofit groups have established PR committees or boards of directors. Rely on their expertise and interest. Don't stop there, however, since you'll want to find out what the public at large thinks, for a less-insulated perspective. Brainstorm for ideas, eliminating none in this initial stage. Upon second review, carefully weed out unrealistic suggestions. Work within a budget. While PR is free (as opposed to advertising), there is a cost for materials and creative time. Whatever you decide, make your plan workable and be open to outcomes you might not have considered previously.

You might be called on to enlist media coverage or support. Media placement remains one of the best-known methods for obtaining good public relations. But the key to successful placement is careful targeting. Don't send a news release out to all media; rather select those reporters with a genuine interest and ability to run coverage or request an interview with your client. If your idea goes against the format of a magazine, for instance, you're wasting your efforts, but if your client is a medical facility and you've cultivated contacts with certain print or broadcast health editors, more power to you. Booking a client as a news or talk show interviewee generates visibility, response to a product or service, and sends a discernible message of credibility as well that often leads to other effective PR opportunities.

Sometimes, you must create opportunities for media coverage. For instance, an executive outplacement company conducts a survey of the city's employment landscape, announces results to the press, and has its name and expertise appear in print. You can disseminate a media guide listing the expertise of your client to inspire coverage. The sponsorship of events often generates publicity or goodwill. Perhaps you can align your client with a media partner. That is a surefire way of obtaining coverage. Also, try the offbeat. Think unique angle such as a company that lowers holiday stress by making neck massages available to employees or shows family-friendly policies by allowing employees to leave a little early on Valentine's Day.

While editorial decisions should not be influenced by advertising, I've seen this occur at smaller publications so often that it's well beyond dispute. At larger newspapers and magazines, editors know better and have their own integrity and the publication's at stake. Smaller publications often survive because of their advertisers. Know who you're dealing with. In some cases, it might be wise to encourage PR clients to take out a small advertisement in a regional newspaper or small magazine to gain favorable editorial coverage, or at least the opportunity to be quoted and listed. The practice runs against all good theory, but, sometimes, reality reigns. Thus, some advertising background or knowledge often pays off for the business writer.

Rely on national directories such as *Bacon's Publicity Checker; Editor & Publisher International Year Book; Standard Rate & Data Service, Inc.;* and *Gale Directory of Publications and Broadcast Media.* Your library should have at least one of these resources.

Reporters rely on PR types to make their jobs easier, but do help, not hinder. Meet deadlines, return phone calls promptly, be familiar with a reporter's beat, and know what story suggestions are appropriate to pitch and which would be absurd. Be respectful of a reporter's time. Don't ask to see stories before they are printed, and don't be a pest by pitching too often. It's a little like crying wolf. When you do have a hot breaking story, you might not be taken seriously.

The *news release* is the standard PR tool for obtaining media coverage. You must offer something with genuine news value; otherwise, call it a *request for coverage* if all you want is a camera crew to show up to create background footage (B-roll) for the evening news.

A request for coverage features the words "who," "what," "when," "where," "why," and "how." Tabbed across from each word is the appropriate information—exactly what busy editors need to decide whether they can or care to cover a specific event.

In a news release, include the same who, what, when, where, why, and how in the lead paragraph. Write in inverted pyramid form. Stick to the facts. Adjectives and sales pitches belong in your sales literature, not in news releases.

It's particularly helpful to quote your client when he or she can offer words of impact, but don't be surprised if a skilled reporter calls for live quotes, not offered to every other media outlet. Avoid all industry jargon, even if your client urges you to keep it in. Keep your writing clear and concise. When ending, use a brief summary paragraph that states who your client is, the basic mission or individual's biographical detail, and anything else that could educate media representatives who are unfamiliar with your client.

In the upper left-hand corner, indicate "For immediate release" or "For release after 10 A.M." You get the idea. Across from that, on the right-hand side, provide a contact (usually yourself, as consultant) and a telephone number where you can be reached or have messages left and/or an e-mail address. Type your news release on your client's (or your PR company's) news release letterhead. Regular stationery will do if you don't have special paper. At the end, use the "—30—" symbol, journalistically recognized as "the end." Be sure to date your release, preferably at the bottom somewhere.

Many news releases are faxed or e-mailed, but just as many are released through regular mail (a week or two in advance for weekly publications; months ahead of time to monthly publications). Ensure that it is addressed to the appropriate editor, and never call to make certain it arrived. Sit back, relax, and pray for a slow news day so that reporters are clamoring for something to cover—hopefully your event or client's news.

With a well-crafted news release, you might create *media information kits* (press kits)—additional staples of PR work. These neatly organized folders (bearing your client's logo on the front) feature inside pockets containing your news release, background sheets, biographies of key players, feature stories that have been written about the organization, charts, logos or graphics, brochures pertaining to your client's work, suggested questions, and captioned photographs. Not every press kit contains the exact same components.

Press kits are handy to have when reporters (or writers like yourself) obtain information. Update and customize them before they leave your office. Some writers don't require photographs, charts, or graphics while newspaper reporters usually will. Different kinds of kits—for magazines, newspapers, and broadcast—save you and your client money.

Creating Collateral Materials and Speeches

Each year, public corporations and nonprofit organizations must produce annual reports for stockholders or contributors. These reports, while sometimes slick and glossy, are being produced with an increasing budget consciousness. An annual report is an honest account of the past fiscal year, with a positive spin. With little jargon, people want to know how the organization has helped others, what makes the company special, what makes it better than others, and what is in store for the future. Sometimes, these reports also include company histories, employee profiles, philanthropy, and corporate initiatives on the environment, education, and health care. You might include a glossary of helpful terms if this helps readers. Annual reports are largely design driven so be certain to review Chapter 11 on other publishing projects. Design elements should be in place before text is created; sometimes the two roles converge. Communication is vital.

Occasionally, you'll be called on to draft speeches for your client whose job is to impress, persuade, sell, entertain, advance a cause, or impart knowledge. Since many loathe public speaking, tap this disdain

Pay Ranges for Business and Technical Writing

Expect to bill from at least $35 per hour for nonprofit PR work to perhaps several hundred (possibly as high as $700 or $800) a day for corporate work. Technical writers charge $50 to $100 per hour or more. Other project rates vary because you have many options when it comes to pricing your services. See the Appendix for helpful professional organizations, such as the International Association of Business Communicators (IABC) and the Society for Technical Communication (STC).

if you have a way with words. Politicians are prime candidates for your writing talent in addition to corporate clientele. You'll need background about your client's style, the intended audience, and the purpose behind the public remarks as you begin your speech writing. Will there be a lectern, a stage, or audiovisual equipment, or will the remarks be more casual? Will the audience be made up of professionals, fellow workers, or people with less or more experience than the speaker?

Find out if your client prefers a word-for-word draft or notes to speak extemporaneously. If you choose the fully written approach, be sure to instruct your client about presentation pointers to keep the effect conversational, so that the speech doesn't turn into a dull reading. Grab listener attention with meaningful statistics, questions, introducing a shocking item, or telling a humorous anecdote. Move from general information to more specific. Wrap up all major points, answering questions you posed, filling in the blanks, and finishing up all stories you began. Here is where the "ask" part comes into play. Ask for the donation, the order, careful consideration, or whatever action you desire.

Audiovisual (AV) writing is often necessary in corporate communications, including many styles, lengths, and formats. These might take on the form of corporate (or nonprofit for that sector) documentaries, miniature histories, promotional or sales videos, or training or motivational presentations. Thinking visually, of course, is an asset. A background in broadcasting or some other area of communication may help carry concepts to the printed page as dialogue, pacing, sound effects, and other facets surface in producing scripts, to be acted out later. Learning software packages such as PowerPoint is also advisable.

Technical Writing

Technical writing and product manuals expand our knowledge, often teaching us how to assemble, use, maintain, or repair something at home or at work. They provide training and staff information, outline various jobs, and specify operating procedures at particular companies—anything print oriented having to do with the specialized areas of science and technology. This broad description includes physical and natural as well as social sciences. Accuracy, brevity, and clear style are hallmarks of excellent technical prose.

Testing for Readability

As a writer, you might be curious to know what grade level you are writing at because it's estimated in some areas that we should aim for a target audience of sixth- to ninth-grade readers. Certainly, a trade journal geared toward those with advanced degrees demands a different writing approach from a technical manual for operating a household appliance.

Many word-processing programs include utilities such as the Flesch-Kincaid Reading Level Index, which gives an estimate of your writing's grade level. I find it to be a little complex, but using a search engine, feel free to look this one up. Other writers use the Gunning-Mueller Fog Index, where you take a sample of at least 100 words. Divide the total number of words in the sample by the number of sentences. This gives the average sentence length of the sample.

Next, count the number of words with three or more syllables in the sample. Don't count capitalized words, combinations of two short words (such as "bookkeeper" or "butterfly"), or verb forms made into three syllables by adding -ed or -es (such as "created" or "trespasses"). Divide the total of these words by the number of words in your sample. If you have 20 long words divided by a sample of 100 words long, then you have 20 percent hard words in your sample. To obtain the Fog Index, add the sentence length and percentage of difficult words. Multiply this total by 0.4. The answer equals the grade level or years of education needed to readily understand your writing sample. Anything over 17 connotes college graduate reading level.

A more widely accepted method is the Fry Readability Scale. Based on a sample passage of your writing, it averages the number of sentences and the number of syllables per 100 words. Your score equals your readability level (grade level)

Occasionally, I'll use a readability index in a business writing class only to prove a point. If you wrote to obtain a favorable index score, your sentences would often lack style by becoming choppy or disjointed. Use these only to spot-check your work if you doubt its complexity.

Technical writers also say it pays to know many different software programs, and that a certificate or master's degree in technical writing may provide opportunities for portfolio samples in addition to contacts that get you started.

Thinking visually is another distinct advantage. In technical writing, a photograph, a diagram, a map, a drawing, a flow chart, a pie or bar chart, a table, or even an equation might describe how something works or looks like far better than mere words. This doesn't imply that you must master these tasks of producing a diagram or creating a stellar chart. It means that you'll likely interface with graphic artists and need to explain the artistic matter.

Use plain language rather than complex, specific versus general. Err to the familiar word, and as much as possible, use terms that readers can visualize. The active voice carries greater weight than the passive. Write in the past tense to describe experimental work and results. Otherwise, err to the present tense. You can find answers to your other style questions with books such as *The Elements of Technical Writing* by Gary Blake and Robert W. Bly.

Creating Manuals

The mandate for manuals is user-friendly text. Poorly written and produced manuals have various hidden costs, on both the user and corporate end, including unnecessary trips to the retailer and calls to technical support lines (thereby raising costs for the company and angst among users), downtime, and lost income. Worst of all, if a product's manual fails to inform and ease the way toward efficient use, it's the saddest product advertisement around. Done well, a manual builds goodwill, reputation, and customer loyalty in repeat brand purchases.

In manual writing, consistency counts. No word diversity or synonyms here. Repetition of key concepts helps the end user. Whenever you introduce new terminology, you're implying a new idea or information. Cut whatever words do not further the reader's understanding. Use the active voice with imperative verbs such as "move," "place," "rotate," "press" or "turn." Finally, manuals are no place for opinion. Just the facts, please.

When you've finished your first draft, test what you've written. Is the reader progressing with each new step? Is he or she confused?

Can the reader find information without an exhaustive search? Is your material still too technical or have you gone to the other extreme of being too simplistic?

Governmental and military facilities as well as private industry frequently require the services of technical writers. These industries include engineering and construction, automotive and aerospace, electronics, biotechnology and robotics firms, computer hardware and software companies, and scientific research and development facilities. If you already work in these areas, but perhaps in a nonwriting capacity, volunteer to take on technical-writing assignments and prove your skills. One experienced writer suggests that you find a company you'd like to write for, and then critique its literature (but not too harshly—the goal is to inspire, not offend). Send this critique with a letter requesting an interview. You might showcase this in a package containing a before-and-after effect, but be careful not to give away too much of your talent. You want the company to be intrigued by your ideas, but need you to fully execute them.

Proposal Development

Proposal generation is a process by which a writer (or team) creates business development or grant proposals to acquire new business or funding for new or already existing projects. In federal and state sectors especially, requests for proposals (RFPs) are common. This differs from technical writing because the focus is more on marketing, but having said that, many advertisements for proposal writers require a range of software proficiency, sometimes listing multiple packages such as WordPerfect or Microsoft Word, PowerPoint, Adobe Pagemaker and Photoshop, QuarkXPress, and Corel Draw, to name a few.

Organizational, research, writing, and editing skills are necessary, as is teamwork because you will interface with many others. In the nonprofit sector, there might not be as many people working on a particular grant proposal, but the same skills apply. Typically a minimum of a bachelor's degree and knowledge of a particular business or industry are required.

One key component to successful proposal writing is to learn as much as possible about those in a position to evaluate the submitted proposal. It's all in the details—whether the business is thriving or

Types of Manuals

Not every manual is created equally. Here are the varieties writers may be called upon to create:

Sales—These manuals list specifications, pricing, and product or service benefits with sales-oriented or more promotional language.

Instructional—These manuals are operation-oriented, outlining procedures to follow to familiarize or master the use of a product, sometimes in a step-by-step manner.

Reference—Explanatory in nature, these manuals seek to detail a function or a feature of a product and are generally meant to have a longer shelf life.

Training—Sometimes sold in packages that contain other items (such as video or audiotapes or CDs), a training manual shows how to get the job done concentrating on task-oriented writing.

Theoretical—These manuals answer the "why" questions that readers or customers ask.

strapped for cash, the success rates and similar projects bid upon, even the company's worst business endeavors. You, of course, won't be adding negative information, but the point is, knowing as much as possible will help you to develop a winning strategy facilitated through writing. Here, more is better than less.

Finally, proposals must address every element requested in the RFP. A table of contents often accompanies many proposals showing how to find the desired information.

Health-Care Writing

Many medical writers work in the pharmaceutical and biotechnology industries, producing regulatory documents, clinical study protocols, investigative drug brochures, marketing material, conference reports, and other materials. Hospitals and health-care organizations use writers and editors for their print needs, including collateral copy, patient handbooks, magazines, and Web site articles.

The potential employer sometimes sets the standards, because some biotech firms prefer to hire scientists who can write while others care more about innate writing ability over scientific degrees. While any health-care writing background can help, including trade publications and Web sites, contract research organizations are good places to gain experience before approaching a biotech firm or pharmaceutical company. It takes persistence and the willingness to pay your dues on less profitable assignments as you gain credibility as a medical/health-care writer.

Like all other specialty areas, writers benefit from the connections they make in national writers' associations. These include the American Medical Writers Association and the National Association of Science Writers.

Starting-Out Steps

Whether it's public relations, business or technical writing, or proposal development, you'll find many opportunities on the nonprofit, government, or corporate horizon. Steady remuneration is one definite perk though you might not work as independently as you might in other writing arenas. Keep in mind the following tips:

- Begin in an industry where you have contacts. Seek other work using telephone directories, building a list of names. Ask satisfied clients for recommendations. Be sure to read upcoming chapters regarding online, newsletter, and desktop-publishing opportunities as well as promotion information found earlier in this book.

- Do your research on current or potential clients. Ask others about their perception of your client. Immerse yourself in the client's world by reading industry publications and checking out competitor Web sites. Maintain an active contact list and periodically touch base with pivotal people to ensure name recognition and a competitive edge.

- Make sure media pitches involve the right proximity (local or national enough), have a people angle (someone well known or with extraordinary challenges), or have a plot (is there a conflict or something of real impact?).

- Consider furthering your education in order to create technical-writing samples to procure work and create before/after samples to impress potential clients. Learn a few software packages and showcase this knowledge on your résumé in order to seek jobs in proposal development.

- Regardless of the business or technical area you work in, be sure to effectively promote yourself and your services. For many, this involves a Web presence, which is discussed in Chapter 10.

CHAPTER 10

Online Markets

ONE OF THE REASONS FOR THE DECLINE IN NEWSSTAND SALES WAS THE dot-com proliferation of online content that continued into the twenty-first century. Newspaper, magazine, and newsletter publishers are only a few of the traditional players. Factor in corporate and non-profit Web pages, personal sites, broadcast news and network Web sites, marketing promotions, product catalogs or e-collateral material, and you will find professionally produced, often well-funded electronic content. This information paradise is a boon for researchers and writers. I'll discuss the possibility of using that research as a job in and of itself later in this chapter.

Otherwise, you can find information on developing e-newsletters and e-books in Chapter 11 and Chapter 12, respectively. Not to exclude these money-making endeavors here, but both topics are so detailed that they deserved their own sections of this book.

Writers have found this fast-growing electronic material market to be just as lucrative as the publications they're accustomed to working for in the traditional print media. The mistake they make, however, is thinking that the skill for one type of writing success easily translates into instant sales in cyberspace. Each medium dictates your writing style and content. This chapter helps you to understand Internet terminology, distinguish the style differences and necessary professional etiquette, and perhaps alert you to any skill retooling or software knowledge you might need to work efficiently and profitably.

There is always another side to any saga, and the collapse of some dot-com stocks proved problematic as the economy turned south in 2001. Many who believed that the World Wide Web was paved with gold lost their millionaire status, and those employees (read writers and content providers) lost jobs as well.

I'm not sharing this to scare you away from exploring online markets, but only mentioning it so that you can wisely forge forward as you select freelance endeavors. Clearly, online presence is pivotal to business success. A Web site, at the very least, lends more credibility to an organization. Few prominent players are without one.

Internet Jargon

Archive—A place on the Internet (or Net) where files are collected and organized for your perusal, sometimes dated many years back.

Browser—Software that enables access to the Internet in a user-friendly format and is able to read photos, text, audio, and video files and present them on the computer screen.

Chat—Talking real time to one another using a chat room or instant-messaging device.

Domain—The three-letter code after your host computer's name in your address (for example, .net, .com, .org, or .edu).

FAQ (Frequently Asked Questions)—Often on Web sites so that people can access answers to commonly asked questions or concerns.

E-book—An electronic book that readers can download onto their handheld computers or hard drives; allows you to access at your leisure with a backlit screen (so you can read in the dark), increase type size, and search the book for a word or passage.

E-mail—Electronic mail sent instantly from one computer to another.

Flame—The act of attacking someone over the Internet, usually the result of spam or for an outright violation of netiquette.

FTP (File Transfer Protocol)—A method of transferring files between computers over the Internet; an area in which users can upload or download files from a host computer.

High-speed access—Refers to a quicker connection to the Internet than using a cable modem or DSL (fast dial-up) connection.

HTML (Hypertext Markup Language)—Otherwise known as the coding that allows browsers to recognize what you've created as a Web page.

ISP—Internet service provider.

Lurker—Someone who "lurks" in an Internet newsgroup without participating; tends to have negative connotation, but it's actually wise to lurk within a group to learn its netiquette prior to posting so as not to offend.

Netiquette—Proper protocol to follow online; a breach of netiquette may also refer to infractions of the Internet subculture, for which many get flamed.

Newsgroup—Formerly referred to as *bulletin boards online*, these groups attract those interested in a particular topic (a writer's newsgroup, for instance).

Server—A special server computer that ladles out data like cooks in a restaurant (for instance, America Online has a server; a company has a server).

Signature file—Permanent characters or description appearing underneath your name, often displaying title, company, telephone and fax numbers, address, or other identifying information.

Spam—Unnecessary waste of Internet bandwidth often in the form of a newsgroup post or an unsolicited e-mail cluttering your online mailbox.

URL—Uniform resource locator that is an address on the World Wide Web (http://www . . .).

Usenet—All the newsgroups on the Internet.

World Wide Web—The most advanced portion of the Internet with graphics, sound, and video; sometimes referred to as the "information superhighway" or simply "the Web."

Seven Caveats of Cyberwriting

1. *Write tight.* Clear and concise. Short and snappy. You've heard the concept many times in this book, but it's even more vital when producing online content. Some print newspapers or magazines run features of several thousand words. Not here. The maximum length that most Web surfers or readers will patiently scroll through might be seven hundred to one thousand words, but more ideal would be in the range of four hundred to six hundred words. If you can use a five-letter word rather than a fifteen-letter synonym, do so. Bulleted lists are great. Start with a verb because this also helps to conserve space.

2. *Think visually.* The e-zine, e-catalog, e-storefront, or e-material you're writing contains a plethora of visual elements. Sure, you might ask if that is extraneous content, but for the most part, everything you see on a professionally produced site serves a purpose. This means multiple links to other sites and content, video clips, sound files, graphics, and more. These still may compete for the reader's attention, however necessary their function.

3. *Study every frame.* Yes, every frame. Just as I recommended that you carefully study a traditional publication before pitching concepts to the editor, the same applies to electronic content. Analyze why links are chosen and what criteria you think earned them this link. Search the archives; look at newsgroups, bulletin boards, reader responses, and posts. Just as you should notice advertisements in a print magazine, you can craft a similar demographic profile by noticing the banners and site ads. Who do you think looks at this site the most? Why? Finally, read any posted writer's guidelines or click on the "about us" icon to learn corporate or organizational history.

4. *Look for writer bylines and editorial contacts.* No bylines? This might mean the publication is not receptive to freelance submissions. No advertising? Well, barring any large, private, or government sources of funding, no advertising on a Web site usually indicates no budget for freelance writers. To find the editor's e-mail address, click on "feedback" or "contact us." When querying electronically, remember to be brief but thorough, and in this case, suggest a few links that you might incorporate into your piece. This will show that you're thinking cyberstyle. Proof of published clips (or in this case links) will show the same.

5. *Remember your netiquette.* Be courteous and restrained in e-mail because this form of communication can come across harsh even when you don't intend for that effect. It is better to lurk long enough in a newsgroup to learn the nature of the discussion before posting yourself. Read the FAQs as well. Never post about a topic that is unrelated to the group's topic. Do not send unsolicited advertising disguised as a post or e-mail. Avoid blind copying others on confidential material because it won't be confidential if they hit the forward button. And always install virus protection on your computer to protect against invaders who can target your address book, thereby harming a colleague's computer.

6. *Be rights conscious.* Just because it's the Internet doesn't mean copyright laws don't apply to downloaded material. In addition, as publishers acquire more rights when they sign writers, recent court rulings have favored freelance writers when publishers transfer writer's print material to electronic databases without their prior consent.

7. *Accept change.* Realize that Web development and electronic content is an ever-evolving process. As society changes, so do trends, needs, and concerns. What you find on a Web site or in the frames of an e-zine will reflect that. The writer who just mastered what the editor wanted might find a new set of requirements in five months. In addition, because content must remain fresh, editors and Web masters are continually putting a fresh spin on a tired topic. Accept this as a challenge and an ever-present part of your online endeavors.

Cyberwriting Style

Use the four "C"s to guide you: clear, concise, correct, and conversational. If you remember these prompts, your writer's voice should naturally shine through. In addition to the four copy requirements, readers want you—a real, living, breathing person—because a personal touch to the text makes anything online (and elsewhere) much warmer to read. Use words such as "you," "we," "us," and "our." Remember creating me-to-you messages in greeting cards? That concept is similar here. Instead of a caption or verse, we're talking entire content that is global enough to appeal to the masses, yet personal enough for the reader to feel involved, to understand the content's relationship to his or her life, and to forget about all the other people scrolling down the screen along with him or her.

When querying, that conversational approach comes into play as well. Instead of writing "Dear Ms. Jones," try "Dear Tracy Jones" if it sounds slightly less formal, or if you're uncertain of the recipient's gender.

Next, make sure you have covered the rest of the journalistic basics, beginning with the lead. It must not only get the reader's attention but the rest of what you write must sustain that attention. Never lose sight of the surfer's temptations. While perusing your content, that reader is just a click away from news and weather; chat rooms; online shopping; or, dare I say, even nude celebrity photos. Talk about competition for the reader's time!

Does this mean that you check your journalistic style at the door in favor of providing entertainment? No, but it does mean a more engaging, lively, less-stilted approach. You're not writing for *The Saturday Evening Post* or *The Atlantic Monthly.* You're writing for a new medium barely ten years old in the height of its popularity. Thus, most Web surfers are of a younger generation, more gadget oriented, a little less patient (that high-speed modem mentality), and they have many more options for their leisure time.

Links become increasingly important in your writing. Before, with traditional print media, you may have relegated other data to footnotes or your own files. Net surfers are used to researching and finding more than they could ever want and probably even need. In terms of a style guide, any underline connotes a link, so don't underline for other purposes.

Single-space using two hard returns between paragraphs. Avoid writing in all CAPS because this is considered to be shouting in cyber-language.

Compatibility Issues

I shouldn't need to say this, but if you aren't connected—electronically speaking—with a computer and personal e-mail account, you have no hopes of making an online sale. Sure, you could use the library's computer, but there will come a time when your editor will want to reach you immediately. If you tell her that you're snowed in and can't get to the public access computers, you will have just committed professional suicide. You should not attempt e-submissions until you have the technology to work proficiently.

Be certain that the editor or publication accepts and encourages e-submissions. Be brief. If you must transmit something lengthy, attach a standard file format (such as Microsoft Word). Some recipients will work off of different computing platforms (PC or Mac) and some may have a hard time opening or reading PDF or Zip files. Some servers will crash if more than one attachment comes through per item of e-mail. That would *not* make a favorable impression, I assure you.

Also blind copy yourself. Some online service providers do not keep a file for sent mail, and if they do, some delete it after a period of time. Save any submissions to your hard disk.

Reslanting Print Material for Online Use

If you read Chapter 6 about article submissions, then you recall that one of the ways to increase your income is to sell reprint rights or to reslant your research for another editor and different audience. Much the same principle applies here, only you're rewriting in cyberstyle for online content.

Be vigilant though. Periodically, I do a search on my name to spot recent publicity or simply to learn what is out there on me (and I sure hope it's all good!). A few years ago, I discovered that a former publisher had posted my work on another topic-related Web site. I called the editor to politely inquire, remarking that I didn't recall ever granting those electronic rights, and pointed out that I'd actually been paid a reprint fee once or twice when evergreen material was reused in the magazine. End result: I received a check for the online material.

The National Writers Union (NWU) recommends that publishers pay writers electronic rights commensurate with what they paid for the use of original or First North American Print Rights. The NWU suggests this because with an international audience in most electronic rights sales, writers stand to lose considerable reprint revenue. If you don't want to hassle with reprint rights as a separate entity, do negotiate a much higher fee for your writing if you sign Web or online rights away. But my best advice is to retain as many rights as possible, and to limit the online use for a specific period of time, from three to twelve months.

Effective Web-Site Planning

If you ask twenty people for their favorite Web site, you'll get that many answers. Web sites are subjective, but there are standards to guide you.

In order that other sites might link to yours, there must be enough information to provide knowledge. Graphically, however, it depends on how that information is displayed. Web users like short bits of information, at least on your home page. From there, they can click around until they're delighted or delirious from content. Thus, have a concept in mind before you begin to craft pages or hire someone else to create a site for you.

Sites such as www.register.com or www.yahoo.com can tell you whether the domain name you've chosen is available. If you can't get the .com version, select another derivative such as .org, .net, or .biz. In fact, if you really want to protect your branding, register all the derivatives of the name with the different extensions. Compare pricing, however, since registering a domain name is competitive.

Long domain names are terribly confusing, and with increased risk of a person misspelling the name, do yourself a favor by selecting something simple. The same goes for selecting words people can pronounce. If they can't say it, chances are good the spelling won't be any better. If direct words can't be used, then opt for words or a phrase that directly relates to your business name or industry. For instance, an optical center might select something such as bettervision.com or brighteyes.com.

Err also to the side of caution regarding Web hosting. While it's becoming easier to host pages from home, problems happen all the time. Go with a company whose reputation you're confident of or ask for references. You don't want the Web-hosting company to go out of business and then scurry to get your site back up and running. Many hosting companies can register multiple domain names. This is important to authors who have many titles and want to choose the same words for domain names as are found in their book titles.

A great feature of having your own domain name is the creation of alias e-mail accounts. These can be set up such as yourname@title ofyourbook.com. Meanwhile, they bounce to wherever you have your regular e-mail account established, and no one is the wiser. But it sure is convenient and professional.

Producing Web Sites

Since most organizations host a Web presence, the savvy writer should learn as much as possible about Web-site development. That doesn't mean you'll become a Web master or content provider. It merely means that you can create a Web presence for yourself if you publish a book or teach a class. Many writers who specialize in business and technical writing maintain Web sites to lessen the costs of mailing information packages describing their services. Asking, "Do you have access to the Web?" often eliminates courier bills or overnight mail. Your site could include writing samples, credentials, an overview of your services, and anything else prospective clients would need to make a hiring decision.

Web pages provide a wonderful, low-cost marketing opportunity. With HTML code, you embed text with tags (commands) for the browser to carry out. Typically, the browser conceals the tags unless you request otherwise. Meta tags contain hidden information inserted into the "head" area of your Web pages. You can maximize your control over how your Web page is described by some search engines with meta tags. They can tell a browser whether a Web page is self-rated for certain age groups or tell the browser what character set to use.

To increase your page coming up on people's searches, include a keyword list in your meta tags. Update these (if you can) every six months so that the spiders of these search engines take a fresh look at your site. (Don't be alarmed by the term, because spiders search out content!) Most search engines compute your ranking based on mathematical formulae, which parse the text, looking for the frequency of search terms, synonyms, and related text, especially at the top of your main page. They generate your ranking based on the search display from that.

Many browsers allow you to look at the code. For instance, in Netscape, you select "view" and then "source" to look at the code. Some Web developers save the code to their hard disk to study what made the Web page work so well. (Mind you, "study," not "copy"!)

You become more marketable yourself to an employer when you have some experience in producing online content and designing Web pages. Developing or maintaining a site in-house also slashes costs.

Among the desirable traits would be a well-rounded liberal arts education, writing and editing experience, and technological aptitude. The more techno-savvy you can make yourself, the better. The same goes for thinking visually. Just don't get too enamored with artwork because graphics make a page top-heavy; that is, they can take a long time to load onto a person's computer, depending on the person's modem speed and connection. There is nothing more annoying than waiting for a Web page you're dying to see, only to have it take five minutes to completely load.

Unless you know that your Web viewers will have high-speed access, develop your content for the end user with a 28K or 56K dial-up connection. Design it for those lower-tech visitors to your site because there are always people operating with older computers and modems, even though many have switched to faster connections. In fact, some users turn off the graphic feature so that pages load with text only. Illustrations typically load faster than photographs.

Rein in your color palette as well. Less is more. Overusing bright colors is monotonous, and reverse text on black backgrounds is difficult to read. Most computer monitors can create a palette of 216 colors. If you use more, the colors may take on a granular appearance as the monitor tries to create the colors by displaying them side by side. This is hard on a viewer's eyes, and there is no guarantee that your viewer will see the exact colors you're specifying. Frequently, the most stunning Web sites use the fewest colors.

Add motion to your site with great care. Imagine trying to focus on text and learn from it while trying to ignore the bouncing balls in the corner or the gyrating logo flashing a name or phrase at you.

Good Web sites clearly communicate content, but the text and the graphic concepts must work together, much the same requirement of newsletters. How do you create that magical balance? Rely on outstanding text more than anything else. Of course, that could be my writing-bent speaking, but I've also known Web masters who won't consider pages as links from their site unless there is a great deal of reference and resource material. That originally was the intention of the Internet—to provide this vast land of plentiful information.

Monitor your Web site and keep it current. Pretend you're a first-time visitor to the site, checking to ensure that graphics load properly and that frames and search boxes display in the appropriate area. Be sure that every link to another page works. If possible, use different browsers to check your Web page. Have friends call it up on their computers. Go to the public library and try to access from there. Keeping current is fairly self-evident. If you click on some organization's page, and you see that it showcases an event that occurred six months ago—well, does that instill much faith in that company? Probably not. If you can't monitor and update your site frequently, for heaven's sake, don't commit dated text to it. Use timeless material. While on this topic, don't lose sight of the fact that this is the *World* Wide Web, not the U.S. Web. Appeal to foreign visitors in your pages whenever possible, but of course, many people don't have the budgets and skills to provide content in various languages. Use your best judgment.

Promote your image, products, or services via your Web-site creation. As some have proclaimed, "If you build it, they will come." The Internet is a first-class promotion vehicle. You're silly if you don't use it to your advantage.

Conducting Online Research

As writers, we search for information, but did you ever think of making money as a researcher? Considering the ease with which we can retrieve information from the Internet, there are plenty of publications, editors, universities, corporations, special-interest groups, government agencies, think tanks, and others willing to pay you to find information that they desire.

Web-Authoring Software

Plenty of software packages exist to help the Web-site designer in creating a compelling site. Products such as Microsoft FrontPage and Adobe Go Live make page development easier, but be sure to purchase a product suited to your level of knowledge and experience. Go Live is created more for the graphic designer or marketing professional who spends limited time on the Web. While I had successfully used Adobe PageMill to create a Web site for myself, I found Go Live to be much more difficult. FrontPage operates much like other Microsoft Office programs, so if you're familiar with these, creating and managing your Web site should be easier. In fact, the program contains customizable themes that you can carry forth throughout your entire Web site. Dreamweaver is another product to make Web design easier, especially for Mac platforms. At this writing, FrontPage is solely for PC users.

Tutorials and specialized books can help the first-time user, but if you can sign up for a class to learn a package, you'll likely learn a lot more. It truly depends on your learning style.

The skills needed include the ability to read and comprehend large quantities of material, write abstracts or summaries based on the voluminous findings, and produce it in a formatted manner. This usually implies a hefty dose of clerical ability, but most writers learn early that this is part of the domain. Competition can be intense at prestigious universities and research centers so be prepared for many applicants for coveted jobs, and also know that advancement depends largely on your credentials. At a university, you'll often feel the pressure to advance toward your own Ph.D. in the process.

On a less scholarly level, you might try various publications, especially those that publish frequently. Editors of these publications can't get enough ideas, science, and studies to back up the editorial and expert opinions. Often, you can do these jobs at home with Internet access and perhaps with the help of library resources. While it's not extremely lucrative work conceiving ideas and finding supportive material for future editorial, it provides steady income while working on other writing projects.

Starting-Out Steps

Plenty of writers have increased their profits by jumping onto the dot-com bandwagon to take advantage of the information superhighway. Familiarize yourself with the terminology used on the Net and carefully study the opportunities and markets for your work. Publishers frequently post guidelines on their Web sites. You can also obtain more information in *Online Markets for Writers: How to Make Money by Selling Your Writing on the Internet* by Anthony and Paul Tedesco. In writing for the Web, remember the following:

- Write concisely with visual appeal. Remember your netiquette.

- Recognize the evolving nature of the Internet, including the changes in technology. Keep abreast of court rulings that affect electronic rights.

- Consider adding Web development to the range of skills you can offer as a writer. Enroll in a class at a local community college, university, or lifelong learning program.

- Maintain a Web page to promote published books.

- Invest in a first-rate Web-authoring software package to guide you if you know little to no HTML coding. If you need to insert an occasional code, consult an HTML guide or study the source code of Web sites that you like.

- Consider earning money as a researcher, even if you're working on longer-length manuscripts but need steady income.

CHAPTER 11

Newsletters and Other Publishing Projects

IN TODAY'S INFORMATION AGE, NEWSLETTERS ARE AMONG THE MANY publishing projects that generate revenue for writers. Other projects generated via desktop-publishing software include brochures and résumés.

While other portions of this book have focused largely on text content, I'll focus more on the look of these publications, while adding some writing advice. Often, you can take advice for one project and use it to create some other printed matter or to breathe fresh air into an exhausted format. You may find the material here provides impetus for change and brainstorming. For fun, don't miss the section on crafting annual holiday newsletters.

Finding Newsletter Opportunities

If you like working with words and graphic concepts, nonprofit or corporate newsletters, church or school publications, e-mailed versions, self-enhancement or image newsletters, even product or service-oriented sales newsletters await. You might also self-publish a newsletter for profit, selling subscriptions to readers interested in a niche topic.

Readers desire information, not fluff. With subscription newsletters, keep graphics and artwork to a minimum or don't use them at all. Price is a subjective matter, for if you price the communications vehicle too low, its perceived value sends a negative message. Price it too high, however, and you'll never attract readers. Careful research is your best bet, and I've listed several publications and organizations to guide the profit-oriented newsletter publisher in the Appendix.

E-mailed newsletters use the subject line to tease the recipient and make him or her open the e-mail. Front-load important content so that your reader will continue to scroll down the screen. Provide links, especially if you desire a certain action. Remember, you're dealing with a point-and-click mentality. Readers want that information at their fingertips—literally. Provide a link that immediately prompts with an order form, asking for payment information and address.

Every newsletter has a large turnover in readers. Tapping into this changing market requires plenty of promotion and reinvesting earnings to attract continual attention to your newsletter, thereby securing additional subscribers.

Why Newsletters Matter

Say you've done some work for a client, and you're looking for ways to turn this client's dormant status into billable activity. Propose a newsletter. First, you must sell higher management on the concept.

In-house newsletters boost morale, keep employees informed, and often serve as public relations vehicles to send to interested media or reporters to generate story ideas and potential media coverage. When produced by a self-employed individual or small group, a newsletter can propel a name into the spotlight. Newsletters remind us of action we need or want to take. Even ABC News knows this: Its e-newsletters from Barbara Walters and John Stossell remind us to watch *20/20*.

Newsletters keep in touch with constituencies. It's not uncommon for churches, congressional members, municipalities, and other groups to rely on them. No other publication, outside of your daily newspaper, conveys as much immediacy and interest. Use all of these reasons when pitching newsletters as potential projects.

Creating Newsletters

What makes a good newsletter? Certainly crisp, clear writing and newsworthy content (there is that word "news" in the title, after all) count heavily. Attractive format follows and a frequency that works for both you and your client. Newsletters, done correctly, are superb, highly targeted public relations vehicles, promoting goodwill to all who read them. Done poorly, they can become a joke and a waste of time, money, and effort.

On the brighter side, marketing newsletters to clients is much easier than selling them on other forms of public relations because they are tangible. When you're finished writing, editing, producing, and printing a newsletter, you have a product to hold up to those who have paid you, and you generally have a mailing list that guarantees a certain level of readership and interest.

Published weekly, semimonthly, monthly, bimonthly, quarterly, semiannually, annually, or e-mailed even daily, most newsletters require at least a quarterly frequency to establish themselves.

Analyze your budget. The more artwork, illustrations, photography, and colors you add only increase the cost of each issue. It's easy to become carried away with your initial enthusiasm. The process, though, begins to drag and turns into drudgery, often grasping for new story ideas when other work takes precedence.

Choose a suitable name—something that quickly and clearly identifies its content and positions your newsletter. It should be professional and easy to pronounce and remember. Aim for something with impact, a powerful word or two that makes just the right impression. Some names build on words that convey a sense of communication—words such as "almanac," "briefing," "digest," "forecast," "outlook," "notes," "spotlight," or "update." I've used the words "connection," "direction," "reporter," "resource," and "quarterly" in titles. Brainstorm through all the alternatives. If you need more than one or two words to convey your message, consider using a subtitle.

Format decisions follow, and most writers choose from a three- or four-column approach for a professional look. There is maximum flexibility, especially for incorporating photography. While a one-column, letter-like newsletter is easy to produce, it's also lackluster. Software allows you to be creative with columns, tool lines, sidebars, clip art, pull quotes, and other elements. Make sure to use that capability to your advantage. Use lots of white space when formatting to avoid a crowded page, and be consistent from issue to issue.

The less is preferable to more approach works here, too. Give a novice fifty different fonts, and he'll use them—all in the same document. The resulting publication looks amateurish. Mailing requirements factor into your format. If you intend to mail the newsletter in an outer envelope, all the page space can be devoted to content. A self-mailer, however, means lost space because of the self-mailing portion, which must meet postal requirements.

Above all, be consistent. We're all drawn to our favorite sections in newspapers or magazines because we know exactly what to expect. We enjoy finding our favorite items in the same place issue to issue, often reading these sections first. As newspaper readers will attest, move the funnies from the entertainment page to the sports section, and you could seriously ruin someone's morning. The key is comfort. Consistency lends that comfort, making happy, eager readers who are ready to peruse the next installment.

When in doubt over any newsletter decisions, establish an advisory panel. Tap the expertise of board members, other employees, or professionals for opinions, for connections with or recommendations for various vendors, and simply as a source for fresh content and editorial planning.

Newsletter-Writing Style

Clear. Concise. Make every word count. If you've read this book as consecutive chapters, you have this concept deeply ingrained into your writer's soul—and style.

When I published a subscription newsletter for a few years, readers complimented me on my brevity, saying that they scoured it as they opened their mail, not days, weeks later when they uncovered it in the "to-be-read" file. This is your ultimate compliment as editor. This is especially important with electronic newsletters.

A newsletter's format is tight and capsulated, allowing for timely information or trustworthy commentary. Many consider *The Kiplinger Washington Letter* (circulated weekly to clients since 1923) to be the granddaddy of all newsletters. "News," however, isn't part of the title, for the publication sells its commentary to an already well-informed readership. If you aren't providing news, then commentary is your purpose.

Regardless, answer the questions of who, what, when, where, why, and how. Make sure people care about your topics. The active voice will help you to conserve prose and convey the coveted sense of immediacy newsletters are known for, while words such as "you" and "your" convey the conversational tone that keeps people reading. When in doubt, read your copy aloud to determine whether it is conversational.

Newsletter Advice to Write By

- Use bullets to show respect for your reader's time and to convey key concepts using a minimum of space.

- Never use the word "free" in teasers for e-newsletters. This often connotes spam and will be deleted by many recipients. Indicate the organization's name at the top of your e-newsletter, close to the subject header because this indicates legitimacy.

- Always repeat any offers or response mechanisms at the close of your e-mailed newsletter. Make it easy for readers to be removed from your list with an unsubscribe link.

- For employee newsletters, focus on the essential six topics, as reported years ago by the International Association of Business Communicators (IABC). These are the organization's plan, personnel policies, productivity improvement, job-related information, promotion opportunities, and the effect of external events on employees' jobs.

- Never allow one clique within an organization to influence all newsletter decisions and content. Provide bylines to offer others' ownership. Conduct a reader survey to ascertain relevant, needed topics. Aim for lateral communication in employee newsletters as opposed to a vertical management-to-staff approach. This builds morale.

- Seek permissions for reprinted items. Copyright laws apply to newsletters.

- Never submit your newsletter for printing without careful proofreading. Another set of eyes spots spelling, content, and graphic design problems.

- Always factor in higher costs for the first issue you create for a client, or submit a separate design fee. Start-ups always take longer. Trust me! Charge separately for inserted material beyond the pages your agreement specifies, and charge extra for rush jobs.

- Never carry your client's printing, paper, or other expenses, but ask that the client establish accounts with these vendors and give authority for you to interface. Nonprofits take advantage of their tax-exempt status, and you'll never be held with a bill that could seriously jeopardize your credit rating, cash flow, and profitability. Shop for the most competitive prices and quality of service.

- Invest in a large monitor if you do a lot of newsletter work because it makes your job less tedious and more accurate.

- Realize that all subscription newsletters will die without aggressive promotion to an ever-changing audience. Prepare to establish a promotional budget.

Newsletter Graphics

Most newsletter designers use one of the popular page layout software packages such as Adobe Pagemaker. Using software takes practice, even a brief course to learn how to fully utilize the product. Your desktop skills will improve with every newsletter you produce. Allow extra time to deliver the first issue for a client.

When adding graphics the old-fashioned way (by T-square and ruler), a drawing board or flat surface will work. White paper suffices for the occasional graphic pasteup. Apply acetate over the blocks where photos will go. Glue down everything with rubber cement, checking for proper placement with a T-square and triangle. Apply a fixative to avoid smudges and secure a tissue overlay on top where you can write any markings to the printer.

Your printer is a valuable resource on how to prepare camera-ready materials, select paper and ink, and more. It might be wise to plan ahead, printing newsletter stationery for future issues, copy fitting all new text into the prescribed spaces. Tell your printer if you plan to feed your paper stock through a photocopy machine or laser printer. It will make a difference in the finish on the paper and in the ink used. I always allow for this flexibility, ordering laser finish stock so that my client or I can print extra copies if necessary. By printing stationery ahead, you only have to plug in the items that change each month, usually in black ink. The key to newsletter presentation is a professional look. Rein in your temptation to use all the graphic arts tools at your disposal and build in plenty of white space to relax the eye.

Reasoned Greetings for the Holiday Season

As sure as you'll see bright lights adorning your neighbors' homes and holly hung from lamp posts, open mail during the holiday season, and you, too, can read all about Aunt Sally's gallbladder surgery or Uncle Howard's home improvements. Oh, those holiday newsletters! If you're producing one for your family, you might want to read this first.

Seems holiday greetings heralding all that has happened in the lives of family and friends have been around for decades, but they've become increasingly popular in our fast-paced society. They're usually created by the family member with the most writing skill and talent; the designated extrovert; or the wildly vain who truly embrace the belief of "all the news they *think* you should know," rather than *need* to know.

Before you assume that I'm against holiday newsletters, I have a confession. I've written my own rendition for as long as I can remember. I began my lighthearted newsletter tradition when few had access to desktop publishing and cut-and-paste graphics, conformed alongside text. And while I sure hope my readers would describe me as a moderately talented extrovert, I'm sure there are a few who roll their eyes, equating my two-page verbiage with a vanity press.

So why do I continue to publish? Simple. While I shudder to think what Miss Manners might say—something like "add a personal note to each carefully handwritten greeting card"—holiday newsletters allow me to impart the past 365 days as succinctly as possible. Key word here: succinctly.

Here are some suggestions for crafting your own holiday newsletters:

Limit the length. Publish a seven-page epistle, and even Santa's jovial chorus will turn into an emphatic "No-no-no!" My rule is two pages (that means one 8½-by-11-inch sheet, front and back). I don't care if our lives rivaled the pages of *People* magazine, it stays at two pages. If it's placed on the "to-be-read" pile, it isn't doing its job. Brevity not only conveys immediacy, but also lowers postage costs.

Gimme the good stuff. Push the positive in those opening paragraphs. Offer something humorous—your best anecdote—to delight friends far away. But if you're like most people, everything in your world hasn't always gone swimmingly. I know. In 1995, a week before Halloween, I found myself suddenly separated, essentially a single mom. The thought crossed my mind to abandon this little journalistic tradition. But what is, well—just is. Why run from it? Interestingly enough, I also used the newsletter technique four years later when a new beau (now husband) entered my life. And that leads to my third tip.

Make it a page turner. Yes, if you want the reader to stick with your newsletter, place a bombshell at the bottom of page one and continue it on the top of page two. Never fails to keep a rapt audience. When I faced divorce, I had several people tell me, "I couldn't believe it when I got to the second page!" When introducing a special someone four years later, I knew friends would be mildly curious. What I gave them in shock value one year I likely made up for in smiles. I gave friends a hint of romance on page one, and let's just say there's good reason that stuff sells magazines.

Deal with events like divorce or serious illness with as positive a spin as you can muster. Focus on being hopeful, or just plain honest. If you don't know how things will turn out, say so. You might even find friends and family rallying behind you with much-needed encouragement and kind gestures. And indeed, even in the worst of times, there is usually something to laugh at. Levity has its advantages.

Stick with the news. Newsletters mean news. It's implicit in the description. There is nothing worse than reading about that gallbladder surgery in full graphic detail or sitting through sister Susan's new decorating scheme, complete with details of the wallpaper print. We have real-life medical dramas and copies of *Martha Stewart Living* if we want that. Concentrate on what people would enjoy hearing about, and tell them something that is worthy of their time. When I peruse a holiday newsletter, I want to learn something that helps me to connect with friends with whom I've lost touch. To read, "The kids are doing wonderfully and getting good grades in school," leaves me wondering "What grade *is* Johnny in these days?" or "What are they doing in their spare time?" Try to think of obvious questions friends might ask if you called them on the phone after being out of touch for hundreds of days. Then write the answers. Take nothing for granted, and be sure to give folks your contact information (especially e-mail addresses if you've switched ISPs).

Focus on yourself and your family. Unless they qualify as a tax deduction, let them write their own newsletter. Give everyone in your immediate family a few sentences in the spotlight. If you're afraid that your own news dominates, watch for the repetitive use of "I," "me," or "my." Then you do have a vanity press operating out of your own home. Having stated this handy rule, I will say there are exceptions. The year I created a stepfamily, I ran brief bios of my new husband's children and my boys. At least a brief mention of important family members, even extended family, makes everyone feel included.

Use sidebars—be creative! Magazines use sidebars all the time. You should, too. Any time you feel yourself veering off topic, use a sidebar to give that tangent a home in your newsletter. Once, I used a sidebar of top-ten quotations—real gems about life over the past year. After moving, I used a humorous take on "you know you've settled in when . . ." Other family members could write a sidebar also. This project is your license to be creative. If you can only muster the energy for a flowing letter with a few headlines, so be it. But if you'd like to pack some pizzazz into your publication, go for it!

Rein in those graphics. There is a vast difference between creativity and wild abandon. Rein in those nifty fonts—not too many please, even if we are having fun here. Same goes for computer-generated clip art. A few well-placed graphic elements help draw the reader into your copy, adding visual appeal. Use subheads, lines, and designs sparingly. Don't dare drop down to 8-point type, either. Studies have shown that older readers strain themselves with anything below a 10-point font.

Allow a child's talent to shine. Here is the place for them to practice their writing and reading skills as they share achievements, special moments, and fun memories. Kids can create entertaining sidebars, artwork, or illustrations, even entire templates for the family newsletter—whatever seems appropriate to their age and abilities. Save these contributions each year, and they'll make precious keepsakes when your children reach adulthood. In fact, each year, I squirrel away a copy of the family newsletter for my two boys as it will be another chronicle of events.

Publish conveniently. It's tempting, in this age of computers and family Web sites, to commit your newsletter to electronic form. That might work, especially if you know that most everyone on your list has e-mail addresses or access to the Web. But invariably, there will be some lost souls who need good old-fashioned paper, and besides, you may want to hang on to copies for those family memories I mentioned. So print several copies on colorful newsletter stationery, or simply on a plain-colored sheet.

Remember those holiday greetings. That is the purpose here, no? Not surprisingly, it's easy to become carried away to the extent that we might forget to wish our friends and family peace, good tidings, and all that good stuff. Invite them to send you their family highlights as well. May your creations silence even the most skeptical of the holiday newsletter critics and have readers anticipating more news that is fit to print next year.

Exploring Other Desktop-Publishing Projects

Like newsletters, many other projects use desktop-publishing software and techniques. For more advanced guidelines, consult graphic design or PR texts, but also follow the advice given for newsletters. Here is more specific advice for three different projects.

Brochures

Whereas newsletters must convey news, a brochure takes on more of a marketing function. Here, you can treat the brochure's cover as an advertisement, using adjectives in addition to information. Desktop publishing allows many formats for brochure design, but the caveat above all is to generate a high-quality promotion vehicle. This can be done without great expense, though color-filled brochures can cost plenty to print.

If you decide to go the color route, choose colors based on desired effect versus personal preference. Your client may love red, but unless you're trying to get the adrenaline pumping to create excitement, your project may demand a more sedate, calming effect that is conveyed in blues (said to elicit the tranquilizing hormones). Green is a comfortable color and often connotes money. Yellow draws attention, but it's not a favorite for some people. White can be dull, but in many circles it's seen as a rather sophisticated choice. Gray is a professional color, sometimes thought to be more exclusive than cream or off-white. Let the project's mission determine the color, but never underestimate the emotional impact adding color to publications can have. Sometimes just varying the rhythm of the color— that is, light pages intermixed with darker ones—captivates readers and holds their attention.

Because a brochure is a marketing piece, don't forget to ask for a desired action. This is why so many brochures incorporate a response, mail-in panel or self-mailer. If not, surround toll-free numbers and/or addresses with tool lines, boxes, or boldface type. Build in plenty of white space and use bullets to your advantage. Our eyes tend to focus immediately on such matter.

Annual Reports

While we covered the text requirements of annual reports in Chapter 9, here we're concerned with graphic concept and design. Many annual reports feature photos and biographies of key executive officers so be sure to have your graphic elements in place *before* you begin any text. Work with any in-house copywriters handling graphics, selecting photos with a balance of ethnic populations, men, and women because you're writing for a diverse audience.

Follow the guidelines for the use of color, knowing that for each color you add to a publication, you're increasing the cost. In a tight economy where dividends have been cut and jobs lost, some companies prefer that their annual reports take an austere approach. Likewise, follow the brochure recommendations for white space, bullets, boxes, headlines, and tool lines.

Résumés

Résumés should be concise, action-oriented vehicles to sell the achievements of the job-seeking candidate—dollar figures produced, funds raised, or percentages of sales and productivity that were increased. Employers like to see signs of self-motivation, accomplishment, and initiative, and they like to see this information quantified. Good writers are usually able to listen attentively, ask thought-provoking questions, and pull just the right information out of their clients. Likewise, a writer proficient at desktop publishing can format this into a visually pleasing document that gets the interviewer's attention. That is what it's all about—getting that special notice that ensures the invitation to interview.

Don't forget military background, educational credentials, outside interests, and special honors or achievements. You'll need to showcase your clients' talents and tap into their hidden skills. This is vital when you're writing a résumé for a career changer or homemaker reentering the workforce after raising a family. Look for ways you can translate everyday tasks we take for granted into bigger skills that if undertaken in the workplace would achieve great recognition. Examples include organizational and budgetary skills, the ability to handle several tasks simultaneously, and effective time management. Volunteer or church-related work comes in handy when your client has taken a leadership role with large groups of people. Including community work is fine as long as you don't overdo it. If you do, the employer may wonder if this candidate has time to devote to a full-time job.

Résumé writing requires that you shed positive light onto bad situations. In cases where someone was dismissed, use phrases such as "will explain personally" or "prefer to keep confidential until interview." If your client works in a creative capacity, the résumé design carries even more weight. Employers will use this as a creative sample, even if you produced it.

Produce two versions of a person's résumé—one to be read electronically as opposed to visually. While one may be sent via postal mail or faxed to a company, the other is likely to be attached as a file or uploaded to a job-search database. The design requirements then vary, as the last thing you want is a format that doesn't convey well. Avoid script, capitalized copy, or the overuse of boldface type. Keep fonts simple and clean. Always check how a client's résumé appears as an attachment, embedded into e-mail text or on a database. Build a fee for any changes into your overall price.

Plenty of résumé books exist. Martin Yate is the author responsible for the Knock Em Dead series. Consult the Appendix for more details on these and other résumé-writing books. Word processing, page layout, and graphics software packages also provide ready-made templates for you to use in creating résumés.

Should your document get too large, beyond the recommended two pages, I'd suggest that you create a separate accomplishments sheet where you or your client can highlight more information.

Starting-Out Steps

Newsletters and desktop-publishing projects can keep the cash flowing into your writing and editing business and become lucrative depending on your set of clients. Be sure to research what others typically charge in your region for these services, and price accordingly. Never carry the expenses of your client. Keep in mind the following tips:

- Keep publications brief, highly targeted, and visually appealing. Consult the journalistic style and public relations subsections in this book for a review if necessary.

- Select a newsletter name that adequately conveys concept. Remember to focus on news or trusted, informed commentary. Aim for comfort and consistency.

✐ Remember that brochures are marketing vehicles, not journalistic ones. They allow greater freedom in word choice because people expect to be sold on a product or service.

✐ Carefully proofread any text or graphic concepts before sending to the printer. It's helpful to prepare a printer's dummy to discuss before making major (costly) mistakes.

✐ Seek clients from the corporate or nonprofit world. Let others know of your résumé-writing services through outplacement firms, colleges, universities, advertisements in student publications, libraries, or online. Convey to potential clients that the cost of a professionally designed résumé is small compared with the lifetime of higher earnings it may garner for the job seeker.

✐ To lighten up your writing projects, try your hand at a holiday newsletter. Involve your children, if appropriate, and let everyone shine and contribute talent. Writing doesn't *always* have to be about generating quick cash. During the holiday season, have a little fun!

CHAPTER 12

The Book Business

THROUGH YEARS OF TEACHING, I'VE HEARD MY SHARE OF BOOK IDEAS, both extraordinary and unrealistic. For writers with a preconceived book, this chapter will guide you in getting the idea on paper and out to an agent or a publisher. For those reading this thinking, "I'll never write a book," I can certainly relate. I thought that once—seven books ago!

Like many nonfiction writers, I wrote to pay the bills but my dream was to write a contemporary novel for women. Off I went to my first writer's conference, where the networking luncheon proved pivotal. One of the two agents attending the conference sat to my right. Upon hearing of my travel assignments, she conveyed how she'd love to represent a honeymoon guide. Wait a minute! I wanted to write fiction. Or did I?

Thoroughly invigorated by a new goal, I followed the advice in a book to draft a proposal. I wish I could tell you that this was my first book sale, but the market wasn't as receptive as we had hoped. What happened, however, was a shift in my focus, now targeting nonfiction books with the confidence that I could craft a convincing proposal. You, too, may find the inspiration for a book project when you least expect it.

Realistic Goals in Book Publishing

Would you spend $28 for a hardcover edition chronicling the life of an ordinary community member? Would you spend $14 on a collection of poems in trade paperback—poems that only resonate with the author and her family? Would you spend $5 to $7 on a paperback novel that broke all genre rules and didn't really live up to competing titles?

Now you have a glimpse of the ideas I field. It's my job, unfortunately, to explain that I once spotted General H. Norman Schwarzkopf's memoirs in the remainder bin, not that long after publication, which means that if his book dropped off in sales, the average person's autobiography might make an even more challenging sell. In one class, a student insisted that I critique her poetry. She just couldn't understand why the local Borders wouldn't stock it. After giving the booklet a look, I suggested that it had merit but needed development if she wanted to self-publish or pitch it to a commercial house. Convinced she had a bestseller, that the Borders's manager and I were nuts, this lady was *not* happy. Also, at my first book signing, a man was adamant that he wanted to pay a publisher despite my telling him that subsidy publishing really wasn't advisable.

So what is a realistic publishing goal? Conceiving a book that appeals to the masses. Remember the "Who cares?" question? Here, if only a few care, all is not lost. You might indeed have a viable self-publishing concept. Plenty of instructors, public speakers, even businesspeople have built-in audiences such as students, people who buy products in the back of the lecture hall, or clients. Also, unless you're crafting a literary novel, it is best to stick to the accepted formula of genre fiction. In other words, don't try to sell the acquiring editor on a romance novel where the hero dies at the end. Sorry, that is not what readers anticipate.

Clearly, some writers have advantages. Those with famous last names frequently bring their celebrity status to the bookshelf, among them business leaders, politicians, public figures, military heroes, and Hollywood legends. Famous names such as Danielle Steel and Stephen King have become literary franchises. Yet even bestsellers fizzle after momentary fame. Everyone in publishing yearns for iconic status.

Other writers who have the right connections move ahead in their careers because of ghostwriting or collaboration, a hot topic, and often an agent to make it all happen. Frequently, writers who have spent years earning a solid journalistic reputation from magazines and newspapers see books as their next logical career step.

Publishing Today

Major publishing houses have not escaped the wave of mergers and acquisitions that pervaded the 1980s and 1990s. They, too, suffered the effects of 9/11. Companies today focus sharply on the bottom line, looking for tighter profit-and-loss margins. Thus, editors carefully acquire projects that must perform. Because of downsizing, editors wear many hats, acquiring literary properties, developing and editing them, plus seeing to business details. With this tremendous workload, it's as if they're looking for reasons *not* to publish a particular project. Those that make it beyond the slush pile had better prove themselves worthy, and fast.

Impress an editor with your grasp and research of a topic. When I wrote the proposal for my book on separation and divorce, I saw practically nothing about separation in the market except one very academic title. Fortunately, my research and idea for a more comforting read paid off. My editor saw the project the same way, and upon double checking my data, agreed. Editors will check your research so you must do a thorough job, especially when researching competing titles and making a case for yours.

There's no other way to gain the sense of history about a book topic—to know what's been written, which books have sold, and what the public wants—without reading widely and falling in love with bookstores and libraries. You build a storehouse of literary knowledge, adding to your understanding of writing styles and commercial successes. Try, as publishers do, to look ahead two years, making an educated guess as to what the public will demand. Sooner or later, you'll find a topic you can call your own—one you're passionate about.

It helps if you offer readers something. They want to become healthier, wealthier, wiser, more attractive, popular, or better established in life. How is your idea different from what already sits on the shelf? Since readers have little disposable time, and publishers must conserve expenses, writers must organize a project concisely, but not so concisely that it is barely a book. Sometimes, what you think is the best book idea is really a series of in-depth magazine articles.

More Than One Way to Write a Book

Not every book has to be a solo creation following the traditional process. There are many other routes to the reader:

- **Turn a vast collection of work into a book.** Magazine and newspaper publishers have done this. If you have columns or articles on a particular topic, this may not be an end result as much as the beginning of a future book.

- **Collaborate on a project if you have the writing skill yet someone else lacks the time and sometimes ability to see a long project through.** Distance doesn't have to be a barrier. When Dr. Tim Murphy (now Congressman Tim Murphy) and I collaborated on a book, technology was 98 percent responsible for our collaboration. Let others know of your interest, especially your agent. Approach experts and those who might have reason to write a book. Look for a coauthor who adds a different dimension to the project, but one who is equally passionate about getting it published. Equal writing talent helps, but sometimes it is the writer's job to bring the expertise to the page. Decide who has ultimate authority over the manuscript or take turns being the lead author on certain sections. Sign an agreement pertaining to work load, deadlines, responsibilities, as well as payment and royalty disbursement, plus cover credit and copyright issues. It's not always a 50-50 split.

- **Ghostwrite.** If you can do without name recognition, craft someone else's story. To keep income high, risk low, avoid speculative work, opting for contracts only. If you don't, you may never be paid. Ghostwriters (they prefer the term *collaborators*) can be paid a flat fee, sometimes much lower than the actual book advance to a celebrity author. In other cases, they share in the advance and royalties. When authors self-publish, they charge an hourly rate, or a chapter or page rate. To protect your financial interests, arrange to be paid one-fourth in advance, one-fourth upon the halfway mark, one-fourth when the project is 75 percent completed, and the remainder on the book's completion.

🖉 **Choose a work-for-hire project.** Increasingly, publishers are trying to keep profits in-house with name recognition in a successful series. Check the copyright to see if it's registered in the publisher's name. Many travel guides are work-for-hire projects in which writers are paid for their work, but do not earn royalties. They may get cover and author credit plus promotional exposure. If you like a certain series book and want to participate, contact the acquisitions editor.

🖉 **Publish an e-book.** Electronic book publishing lured Stephen King to pursue this path, but then again, he can afford large expenses associated with Web hosting and maintenance. As Richard Curtis and William Thomas Quick ask in *How to Get Your E-Book Published*, can you afford similar? This technology is so new that it's discussed further into this chapter.

"Do You Have an Agent?"

Attend any writer's conference, and that's the question you'll hear. What writers ought to ask is: "Do you really need an agent? Are you truly ready for one?"

Writers frequently feel they need an agent to see them through a particular project, but really, the time to seek representation is on completion of the best project you can possibly write. For novelists, this means completing the entire draft and synopsis. In nonfiction, it means a well-written proposal and at least one sample chapter.

Agents serve purposes far beyond representation. Agents are authors' advocates, interceding on their behalf. They take on projects, sell them to publishers, negotiate contracts, and strike the best deals possible. They can guide your career, shape your work, and champion your causes. An agent/author relationship is a business partnership that if successful lasts throughout an author's career.

An agent is one of the few people with honest feedback because he or she works on commission—incentive enough to wrangle you as much money as your writing can command. If you don't make money, neither does your agent. Agents can also ensure that you'll get a fair read. This certainly beats languishing in the slush pile, and post-9/11, publishers now deem agents a critical first screen against bioterrorism.

Agents, however, cannot sell manuscripts or proposal ideas that are not salable to begin with. An agent can shop a project, but not guarantee a sale. Your talent and original idea stand alone.

Agents also cannot command outrageous sums of money—or even much money—for beginning authors, so forget the notion that you can retire after one book. An agent cannot promote your book, play best friend, lend you money, solve your legal affairs or personal crises. Seek out publicists, bankers, attorneys, and psychologists if the need arises.

Finally, an agent cannot sacrifice great amounts of time on unpublished writers. Understand the agent's food chain. At the top are advances and royalty checks; underneath are editors, contract negotiations, and completed manuscripts sent in by published authors. Following down are multibook contract authors, completed manuscripts with potential, unpublished authors whose books have been at the publisher for a week, unpublished marginal authors, and unsolicited manuscripts. Where do you fit into this chain?

Since agents also navigate the slush pile, rejection letters find their way into writers' mailboxes. Agents don't sit around thinking of cruel ways to fend off starving artists. Like you, they face rejection every day. Keep this in perspective, and know that the competition to find representation is stiff. Agents cannot handle everything you write, including articles, greeting cards, short stories, and poetry. You must sell these.

Perhaps you can successfully market your work and strike suitable deals yourself. Perhaps you like one publishing house, and it's a literary marriage that works. Three is a crowd, in other words. I know novelists married to attorneys who look over their contracts, and nonfiction authors who never use agents. Some writers like the excitement of the sale, and they've developed the business acumen to negotiate agreements. Only approach an agent if you're convinced one can help and only when your work is polished, your attitude professional, and your expectations realistic.

Ask published authors who represents them, and whether you can approach this person by way of referral. Never use an author's name unless given express permission to do so. Agents frequent writer's conferences with hopes of meeting clients with prolific potential. People connect with other people. Only then do they get turned on to ideas. If you have the opportunity to meet an agent and discuss your writing, that is great. If there is a book that you particularly admire, call up the publishing house and ask who represented it. If you're already published, but remain unagented, your editor can suggest agents for you to contact regarding future projects.

Otherwise, use directories that list agents and their expertise. *Writer's Guide to Book Editors, Publishers and Literary Agents* by Jeff Herman and *Writer's Digest*'s *Guide to Literary Agents* are my favorites. Both are annually updated and very detailed, but Herman's is a book you shouldn't be without if you market to book publishers.

Resist the urge to sign with the first agent. Research each one to discover his or her specialization. Don't waste your time with agents who deal only in fiction if you wrote a self-help book. Ask for a list of recent sales and clients to determine their satisfaction with the agent's performance.

Inquire about policies and fees charged, if any. Will the contract cover one project or all of your writing for a stated period of time? Some agents charge reading fees and others do not. Directories usually list these two types separately. Most agents will expect reimbursement for expenses they incur representing your work, including heavy volumes of photocopies, messenger services, or overnight deliveries. Whether to sign on with an agent who charges a reading fee is, at times, hotly debated among writers. Agents who charge fees do so to cover the overhead costs of running their businesses. Others frown upon the practice. You must feel comfortable. Steer clear of anyone who doesn't instill trust and confidence.

As in all relationships, two parties join together with high hopes. Agents want to make authors successful, selling every project. Authors want to work with, not against, the advice of their agents. But sometimes there are signs that the agent/author relationship isn't working.

Among these bad omens: Your agent does not respond to your queries, submissions, or telephone calls within a reasonable period of time (a few weeks to a month). Agents cannot spend time hand-holding clients. Unfortunately, this is exactly what many beginning writers demand. Reporting to you on a too-frequent basis uses up time, energy, letterhead, and postage that could be better spent marketing your work to editors and publishers. If you constantly have to remind your agent about outstanding queries or manuscripts, you have reason for concern. Other reasons to question the relationship: failure to pay advances and royalties promptly or undue pressure to pay for elaborate editorial or rewrite services to guarantee a sale. There are no guarantees. Steer clear of disreputable editorial services that prey on unsuspecting authors.

While there is no great way to break off the agent/author relationship, it's best done professionally and in writing. Refrain from airing any dirty laundry. Withdraw your work from representation and do thank your agent for the time and energy devoted to your work. Politeness lasts forever in all businesses, certainly in one as communications oriented as publishing.

How to Write a Book Proposal

Nonfiction is easier to sell because it begins as a proposal. You need not write the entire manuscript. In fact, you shouldn't. Editors and others on the publication board want to help shape the book. Expertise also makes nonfiction an easier sell because you can impress your publisher with wisdom and insight. If necessary, collaboration works to see the book through, but of course, a combination of expertise and writing skill is a better ticket to your publishing dreams.

Begin your proposal with an introduction. This is called the *overview* or brief description of your idea. Here is the hook—the selling line. Sometimes, I've incorporated the question "why this book" into the proposal, using those words instead of "overview." It does the same thing, essentially summarizing the book's mission. Why do people need, or think they need, your book? Answer the question, "Why now?" Expand that mission into a few paragraphs. Focus on the book's purpose, approach, organization, and content.

Will your book require a *foreword* or *introduction*? Alert potential publishers to anyone who could contribute this, especially if this person's name would be a valuable cover credit. Continue to think through the project so that you can write a paragraph regarding your book's *back matter,* including the index, glossaries, and appendices.

If there are any *legal* or *technical considerations* that may need untangling, address these. This is where you mention necessary photographs or graphics. Also include a suggested word or page count because publishers need to know how vast the material is in order to factor their production costs.

Who will buy this book? Include these groups under *potential markets*. Think broadly, beyond the average bookstore crowd. A lawn-care book can sell at Lowe's or Home Depot. A pregnancy book can be marketed at pharmacies, warehouse clubs, and maternity shops.

Devote a page to the *competition surrounding your book*. You must be able to present title, author, publisher, publication date, length, core focus, and how it's different from the concept you're presenting. Don't fret too much over the competition. Trust me, you want some competing titles or else the editorial board may view your idea as a niche topic that won't sell. On the other hand, if you see dozens of already existing titles, you may want to reconsider or reslant the project.

What *promotional outlets* do you have in mind? Discuss the ways you can innovatively sell your book through public speaking, teaching, interviews, or writing articles, to name only a few. If you know of experts, celebrities, or others whose endorsement would enhance the salability of your book, include these. Publishers want media-savvy authors.

Sometimes you should include a page titled *resources needed to complete this book*. Use this only for extraordinary expenses such as travel, excessive and long-distance telephone interviews, and surveys you must conduct. Additional expense money is a rarity, and authors generally write off incidental expenses as their own costs of doing business.

You get to shine on the *about the author* page, with pertinent facts about yourself—previous jobs, special connections, and years of experience or education that make you stand apart from others.

Chapter outlines are crucial. In some proposals, I've ganged these two or three chapters to a page; in others, I've devoted an entire page to a single chapter. Outlines take on a narrative style. No Roman numerals here, though I've found that bullets work well to convey content. Other times, paragraphs work best.

Sample chapters represent your skill and organizational ability. Most proposals contain at least one chapter to show how you intend to develop the material, how you connect with and engage the reader. Give it all you've got. That first chapter will hook one editor, who in turn takes the project to colleagues on the editorial board. These people will vote for or against your idea, sometimes sending the editor back with unanswered questions and a healthy dose of interest. When you spot an editor's enthusiasm, work even harder to shape the proposal into something spectacular. *Writing samples* usually mean articles, columns, small booklets, or commercial projects that you have written in addition to that sample chapter.

Assemble all of these proposal components into a two-pocket folder. Writing samples go in the left pocket along with reviews or endorsements of your work. On the right side, place proposal contents including sample chapters. Proposal length truly varies from a few pages to a proposal of two dozen pages or more. Center a plain white label with the proposed title of your book and your name on the outside of this folder. Insert a business card into the perforations provided in most folders.

Writing Your First Nonfiction Book

First books are much like first children. We see no wrong in them, at least at first. Soon we tame them just as we might our offspring. For sure, we must protect them.

After signing every book contract, I've had that momentary panic as in "Oh, my—now I have to write the thing!" I've found that the most helpful guide during the writing stage is the proposal that initially sold the project. Many times, I've simply followed this chapter by chapter. If I came upon a section of material that required more in-depth research, I inserted "MORE TK" into the manuscript so that I could do an easy search-and-find and insert later.

Always end a writing session by backing up onto disk or burning a CD. Saving the material as another version (by creation date, such as book12.20.doc) prevents any mishaps. Use the "save as" function to prevent copying over an older version you might need. When doing book projects, safeguard an electronic version in a safe deposit box. The thought of re-creating an important, time-consuming work daunts most authors and warrants the precaution.

Try not to edit as you write. Perhaps halfway through a book, if you

The Mystery of Book Advances

Determining a book's advance is one of the most arbitrary decisions in the business. The money a publisher is willing to advance against royalties clearly indicates the project's perceived value, the marketing commitment, its place on the publisher's list, and the publisher's resources. Typically, smaller (including religious) publishers and university presses do not have the capital to speculate with, so they offer meager advances. Sometimes, they make up for a paltry advance with a more generous royalty clause.

At this writing, for a small or university press, we're talking under $5,000 for a first nonfiction book. Midrange publishers offer $5,000 to $10,000, and larger houses will be more competitive. Work-for-hire guidebooks generally command a flat rate of $8,000 to $12,000. Collaborating with another author doesn't automatically mean more money. A strong record of nonfiction writing (and healthy prior book sales) in addition to expertise, status, topic relevance, and promotional ability can boost these numbers.

Some agents will put a proposal out to auction, meaning that publishers are invited to bid against one another to established ground rules. Sometimes a proposal will sell to the highest bidder, but since your agent's job is to find not only a good publisher and contract but also a good editor, you might need to review all facets of the offer for the best publishing environment. Auctions are the exception, not the rule. You must give acquisition editors several weeks to two months to review your proposal, sometimes longer. Multiple submissions are the norm in pitching proposals, but you should always target them to a particular editor.

are worried that you're coming in over the projected word count, then you could print out a few chapters and tinker. Generally, I leave tinkering to the very end, after I've created an entire first draft. The stress is much less, and it's easier to edit my own work.

Seek permissions along the way because you must turn these in with your completed manuscript. In fact, beginning writers should keep permissions to a minimum since the author often pays for these if not granted at no charge. Check and double-check facts, and don't overlook the introduction, appendices, and index if you're responsible for these segments of the book. Though I'll discuss book promotion shortly, write with promotional possibilities in mind. Knowing that editors love sidebars to published articles and that on-air talent love bullets to read aloud, I often format sidebars or insert fun material (like the holiday newsletter tips in Chapter 11) with intriguing information that could also be presented in future press kits, thereby enticing media coverage.

Once you've written your final manuscript, resist the urge to marry it. Put some distance between yourself and the final edit if your deadline allows. You're more likely to find any last-minute errors. Print it out and prepare a disk or CD for your editor (according to your contract).

Hopefully, your content editor will call for a light copyedit, whereby the copyeditor line edits for grammar and spelling, for the most part. If your book requires a heavy edit, it is best to offer to trim and produce this yourself, lest an editor remove not only material but also your written voice.

You'll see the project several times before the final galleys, but when these hit your doorstep, you must act fast to review and return them. Too many changes at this point will cost you financially, as it's expensive to change much material at this stage.

Writing Children's Books

Please don't think that just because children are smaller and still growing in intellect, writing for them is any easier. It isn't. In fact, the competition can be fierce. Reviewers and librarians carefully critique thousands of children's books each year, though opportunities abound.

Do you have a healthy dose of a child's curiosity and concern about the world? If so, you might be perfectly suited to craft children's nonfiction (or fiction) books.

Editors caution beginning writers *not* to base their children's tales on their own son's or daughter's antics. What may appear cute at the family picnic won't necessarily translate well in print. Instead, use the humorous incident to inspire a more in-depth story line. Since children are known for their rampant curiosity, use your own child's questions to inspire a nonfiction concept.

Relevance is critical. Kids have grown more sophisticated these days. Forget fooling them with a fantasy world that doesn't include teen romance, divorce, the search for world peace, and other modern-day concerns. Editors ask children's authors to experience situations from a child's perspective. Especially for younger kids, how would you feel always looking up to a person towering above you? Or what if you could never reach what grown-ups easily retrieve? Kids like to see peers as the lead characters, not the sage grandpa with all life's answers. Situations *and* words must be relevant so structure the book's vocabulary to a child's specific age.

Syl Sobel, author of nonfiction works including *How the U.S. Government Works* and *Our Pledge of Allegiance,* advises writers to write about things they like and know. This way, your enthusiasm will shine through. Sobel's background is in newspaper and law, and he works for a government agency in Washington, D.C. "It's helpful to think of nonfiction as a conversation with your reader," he says. "You're explaining something to a child. Think about the questions he or she might ask, and answer each in terms the child will understand."

Make your subject come alive. As Sobel writes about history, he uses facts and anecdotes to make history (and characters) seem real, and he explains the subject's significance on people's lives. Children want to know how things affect them. Sobel adds, "If you can find humor in your topic, bring it in. If there's some opportunity to get close to silly, that's fine too. Don't let humor overshadow your topic's significance, but don't avoid it either." Humor can hold a child's interest, and parents reading with children appreciate that just as much.

If you're crafting a child's fictional tale, cover all the aspects of any novel—hooking your reader, creating conflict, reaching a climax, and bringing your story to closure. Very young children have even shorter attention spans, so your hook must be quick. Young readers are much more interested in what is happening now, tomorrow, or next week than they are in what took place in the past. Use literary devices such as the flashback and time lapse sparingly since they grind the action to a halt.

Watch the tendency to bring animals to life. While some bestselling authors have successfully anthropomorphized bears, bunnies, and turtles, writers have come to overly rely on this device to everyone's detriment. When an editor spots this device, he or she is more likely to toss the manuscript aside, thinking, "Oh, just another dancing dinosaur."

Beware of contrived endings that skew reality for children. As I indicated, children today deal with real, sometimes harsh issues. Children don't like to be lied to, and they truly are savvier than most people realize.

Writing and Selling Novels

While I can juxtapose facts, interviews, trivia, and much more in the nonfiction realm, I'm truly impressed by writers who can weave a good tale, without benefit of already existing characters and plot. Fiction writers rely primarily on their vivid imaginations with some research. Good fiction entertains but also informs. The novelist weaves important information about the world as he or she tells us about the make-believe story.

The opportunities in fiction include short stories; screenplays; romance, mystery, horror, adventure, western, and science fiction novels; and children's literature. All fiction requires imagination and a capacity for storytelling. The writer's job is to build suspense, create curiosity, and foster a sense of worry or dread. Without these essential elements, you will not produce the page-turner that editors, publishers, and readers require.

Unlike nonfiction where you can sell on proposal and sample chapters, you must create the entire manuscript. It's impossible to pitch a novel intimating how romantic, how funny, or how spine tingling it will be. The agent and ultimately the editor must read it from page one to conclusion.

What you submit to an agent or editor must be the best work you can possibly create. Revision is your first selling tool. If necessary, learn to delete entire scenes, eliminate characters who serve no purpose, and cut dialogue that doesn't move the story forward. Know your market and follow the publisher's guidelines. Don't argue with your editor to disregard genre rules. Only after you become a top-selling author can you take chances like that.

The Novel Synopsis = Selling Tool

To understand the significance of the synopsis, let's put it into this analogy: The synopsis is to the novel what the proposal is to a nonfiction project. It's vitally important to the sale of your work.

Why invest the effort in this when your novel must be judged as a whole anyway? Agents and editors cannot read your entire manuscript from start to finish. A synopsis does the selling for you. This narrative summary of your main action can range from two to ten pages. It should be double spaced, professionally typed, and painstakingly precise.

Begin your synopsis where the story excitement starts. Don't spend valuable time giving too much background that elicits a yawn before the editor even gets going. You want your opening to be bold, full of conflict. You want it to hook the editor into requesting your completed manuscript.

Write your synopsis in the present tense and in the third person. Its form should be that of a running story, rather than chapter-by-chapter details. If you write "this happened, and then that happened . . . ," your synopsis will become a poor reflection of your abilities.

Keep action at the center, outlining the protagonist's problems and how they escalate throughout the remainder of your book. You must include the climactic scene and tell how the story is resolved. No editor will request your manuscript unless he or she has a feel for the entire read ahead of time. So don't hesitate or hint. Write your conclusion concisely. If you've never written a synopsis before, read books that share a successful synopsis that sold a manuscript.

Use an agent specializing in fiction. If your career comprises both nonfiction and fiction writing, consider having two agents if you cannot find one to satisfy all your needs. Some feel that authors need overall career guidance and could get lost in the shuffle between two business partners reviewing work and making deals. That decision rests with you.

Highlights of Good Fiction

Your book begins on page one, paragraph one. If your editor can't get past these components and finish the first chapter without yearning for more, your book is doomed from the start. All too often beginning writers introduce three or four characters at the outset, hinting at their relationships, making them exchange a few lines of dialogue and embroiling them in some sort of drama. Other times, they open with narrative that tells the story, leaving the reader to search for the main character he's meant to fight for and follow. Neither is good technique. Too much detail all at once involves telling rather than showing—the kiss of death in fiction.

Your fictional account must showcase your main character, giving the reader someone to focus on. If your main character can't be in the initial scene, then someone needs to carry the action until your main character is revealed (and you had better do this soon). In novels, you have a little more leisure by which you can introduce main characters; in a short story, these people should turn up immediately.

Create characters that your readers can root for, not stock characters perpetrating stereotypes. Look at the world around you. Is everyone in your inner circle of friends and acquaintances the same? Of course not. Life would be a bore, and so will your fiction if you follow this stereotypical path. Instead, give your characters positive traits as well as weaknesses. Get inside a character's head, knowing what sends him or her soaring in happiness or plunging into depths of depression. Allow human choices that lead to joy or sorrow. Create a character chart to develop and keep track of your character's education, previous jobs, ambitions, religious beliefs, special memories, mannerisms, phobias or secrets, hobbies, and hidden talents. You may never need all the details you sketch, but they help you to develop multidimensional characters. Allow characters to grow. This keeps the story moving forward. What does your character want? Make the reader want that for him or her. We call this motivation, and you should provide enough detail so that readers keep turning the pages.

Action is everything. So is word choice. Use words that describe rather than judge. If a woman has unattractive hair, you might call it "tangled" instead of "ugly." That description is more concrete and rich in meaning.

Plot is also pivotal. Imagine life without adversity where everyone got along, families never fought, everyone fulfilled their dreams, and nature never took sudden twists and turns that changed peoples' lives. Your first paragraph cries for conflict. Your characters could compete with one another. They could battle nature or struggle within themselves, but no matter what type of conflict you enlist, you owe it to the reader to introduce it early.

Know where your story is going and how it will end, before you even write it. Many beginning fiction writers look upon plotting their novels as sheer drudgery, but plotting resembles a motor club route all mapped out. It's a help not a hindrance.

If you get bogged down, ask "what if" questions and write down the answers until you discover an idea that works. Place your character out of his or her element, a surefire way of introducing trouble. Decide what effect you want your reader to have upon finishing your story. Or, draw a visual diagram of the characters and events. Just make sure that whatever occurs feels natural. Your characters are not puppets you manipulate on a whim.

Introduce subplots in longer-length fiction. These plots use secondary characters who are well defined but do not take over the story. Your minor characters interact with your primary players, allowing them to show the full depth of their personalities—the good and the bad we discussed earlier. Subplots can mirror the main action or keep the story in motion, while the main plot rests for a while. Introduce your first subplot as soon as your main plot is established. Carry it through, to the conclusion of the book, if you like, but wrap it up before the main plot.

Scenes and dialogue both work to progress your plot. Dialogue is one of your best tools for showing, not telling. Consult your character chart, and allow each one to use favorite expressions, local dialect, or familiar slips of grammar if these are in keeping with the character's overall personality. If you ever doubt that your dialogue is realistic, read it aloud. If it sounds unnatural, rework it until it flows like an ordinary conversation.

Also, don't hesitate, as many beginners do, to use the word "said" when attributing dialogue. Don't write: "I love you," she smiled. People don't smile their sentences, so use words that convey speech, not bodily action.

The Truth About Subsidy Publishing

In the back of many magazines, you'll often spot advertisements calling for book-length manuscripts. "Pay us to publish your book," they promise. Such an offer sparks a ray of hope. Unfortunately, that spark often fizzles to frustration when writers become involved with subsidy publishing.

Most publishers make their money selling books. Some publishers—called vanity presses—make their money by charging authors to publish their manuscripts. Publishers should have a vested interest in your success as an author and in your book's sales record. If you and your books succeed, publishers should see a sizeable return on their investment. Vanity presses have no vested interest in the success of either. They've already made their money—from you, not on the work's sales. What incentive do these companies have to do a stellar job? Very little, I'm afraid.

Vanity publishing is completely legal, but few, if any, bookstores or libraries purchase vanity-published books. In fact, vanity publishing usually has a negative impact on a writer's career. Frequently, writers pay large sums of money to have their books printed, and the results are often disappointing. If any promotion takes place, it's at the author's expense. The entire process is filled with uncertainty and financial risk.

Self-Publishing—A Viable Alternative

I spoke earlier of having a niche topic that you might feel comfortable self-publishing, especially if you have potential back-of-the-room sales at speaking or teaching engagements, or a particular client base. Self-publishing isn't subsidy publishing. At the surface, the two may seem similar—you're still footing the bill. But in self-publishing, you provide the capital and maintain control over the process. You do everything the publisher would, in addition to the author's role.

Some self-publishers deal strictly through mail order. Others use small book distributors to gain access into retail bookstores. Still others market their books through a combination of the two techniques. Before you go this route, spend some time researching this process, just as you would if buying into a franchise. If you thought writing a book was a challenge, just wait until you prepare, produce, print, and promote every single word you write. Look in the Appendix for resources to guide you in producing nothing less than professionally written and designed books. If you skimp on quality, your readers won't be fooled. You'll likely need to hire editing, design, layout, illustration, photography, printing, binding, and distribution services. Talk to other self-publishers to find out what they've learned over the years. If you decide to self-publish, establish a company name to add legitimacy. Sometimes, self-publishers prove an existing audience (with a solid track record of consistent sales), then shop the rights to a commercial publishing house to keep the book in print and obtain an advance along with future royalties.

Print-on-Demand Publishing

For a fee, some publishers with new print-on-demand (POD) technology will digitize your manuscript, create a cover, and list the e-book with an official ISBN at prominent online bookstores. When a reader points and clicks, printers many times the size of an office photocopy machine literally roll the manuscript off the presses, and the book is then mailed out within days. No more attic loads of books that you wonder if you'll ever sell. No more books gone out of print, to never touch a reader's life again. If the rights of your out-of-print project revert to you, print-on-demand publishing allows you to digitize and be back in business, earning further royalties whenever a reader buys your book.

Xlibris and iUniverse are two of the largest POD services. They aren't publishers in the traditional sense, but purveyors to publishing. For a fee (ranging from $99 to more than $1,000), anyone can be published and earn a royalty on sales. Now, isn't this the same as subsidy publishing or self-publishing? In some aspects, yes. Read on for some important distinctions.

With fee-based PODs, the author selects from services the company offers, whereas a self-publisher controls the process. Self-publishers keep all proceeds and maintain all rights, but with PODs, authors are generally paid only in royalties, and the rights often go to the POD service, at least for a specified period. Does this smack of vanity publishing? Yes. No doubt this form of publishing isn't perceived as the traditional path to print.

On the plus side, because the book business operates on a full returns policy, authors can sidestep a publisher's "reserves against returns" standard in contracts. This means that a percentage of author earnings is withheld against potential returns. Books must sell through this, which means the equation resembling books shipped minus books returned/unsold equals the sell-through figure. In traditional publishing, fewer than half the books printed may sell. So with e-publishing, the sell-through can approach 100 percent. That's pretty good.

On the down side, there are higher unit costs associated with e-books. Readers may balk at a $30 price for a book they're generally accustomed to buying for under $18. The primary focus of these companies is selling a service to you, not in selling your book to readers. If you have an out-of-print work, however, it may be to your advantage to get your book back into circulation at minimal cost through e-publishing. If you're a writer just starting out with a new project, know that because PODs closely resemble subsidy agreements, readers, reviewers, and booksellers may shy away.

Before entering into such arrangements, closely examine the package as proposed on the company's Web site. Look for additional charges that aren't included in the initial package, such as cover design, applying for copyright, and obtaining an ISBN. These fees can add up to disappointment. The contract should have clauses with clearly defined royalty rates, provisions for reverting rights back to the author, and protecting excerpts only with your express permission to print these again. You, as author, should be able to terminate the agreement, and you should be careful what options and financial stakes you grant to future works

Book Promotion

You've spent months, maybe even years, writing a book and working with your editor through the production process. Now your work is over, right? Wrong. You have a product, and your ability to hustle it will determine its future, and your financial take on it.

As a first-time author, you won't get much publicity support beyond a press release, catalog copy, and some interview pitches for a few weeks out of the gate. Then, the onus falls to you to keep your name circulating, offering to appear in print or on talk shows. Work with your publicity director, promptly returning author questionnaires and anything else that is requested. Alert your publicist to any special audience, market, or promotional opportunities.

Word of mouth begins with yours. Let everyone know that you've written a book. Write to your alumni publication, former professors, professional associations, and certainly to newspaper and magazine editors or talk-show producers. Write articles or offer excerpts in advance of publication. Send reporters and talk-show hosts a list of questions or those excerpts (sidebars) I mentioned earlier. This just might ensure that you're booked as a guest.

Offer to speak before conferences, community groups, or gatherings of concerned citizens. Inform your publisher at least six weeks in advance of a speaking engagement so that sufficient copies of your book can be on hand for attendees to purchase. Bring a friend along or arrange for help in collecting money and selling your books.

Bookstore managers often welcome authors who want to sign their books because events draw customers to the store. Many of the big chains, however, have opted out of signings, and some no longer have community relations coordinators to set up events. If your subject matter lends itself to maternity boutiques, sports departments, toy stores, or gourmet shops, book events there.

Starting-Out Steps

Publishing books as a business has undergone both positive and negative changes. It's exciting to see a body of research or the best displays of your imagination bound together between two covers. With today's technology, make that downloaded within seconds or printed on demand. Like anything else, do your homework first. Sometimes, this resembles a crystal ball as you forecast what readers will want and need two years hence. Keep in mind the following tips:

- Invest the time in a well-crafted nonfiction proposal and sample chapter or a novel synopsis. These selling tools can help determine a publisher's offer or rejection.
- Suggest a nonfiction project to corporate clients or as a premium deal with the book as an incentive gift to attract business. Any time you can guarantee large quantities of sales, you'll have an easier time finding a publisher.
- Stick to the accepted formulae of genre fiction. Show, don't tell.

Seven Ways to Sell Even More Books

1. **Offer an index.** Studies show they boost sales.

2. **Prepare your own author bio and jacket copy.** An employee who may never have read your book might write cover copy. Leave nothing to chance.

3. **Create innovative special events.** Cookbook authors might prepare samples of their recipes to serve on trays at a book signing or speaking engagement. Ask catalogs to carry your product, if related. (Through persistence, I got *The Angry Child* into the A.D.D. Warehouse catalog and Web site.)

4. **Always sign books because once autographed, books cannot be returned to your publisher.** (Remember that sell-through equation.) If you self-publish, slip an order form into your book, or devote a page in the back matter for future orders. Readers will often recommend books.

5. **Get to know your publisher's sales force.** Offer to write a memo to the publisher's sales staff introducing yourself and your topic and offering assistance. Any extra information helps them sell your book. Ask your editor if you could speak before the sales force at the annual sales conference or book convention, where sales representatives learn of new releases.

6. **Speak in sound bites.** A blurb is a short statement about a topic. Have one. Have several. Be ready to articulate them whenever called upon. The best scenario would be on a top-rated talk show with the power of *Oprah!*.

7. **Cultivate relationships with the media.** Let them know you're available to comment on breaking news or seasonal topics. My book *Surviving Separation and Divorce* does well during holidays because people are lonely and in need of friendly assistance.

✐ Write children's books with illustrations in mind. Pictures make up at least half the content. Include sensory detail relating to the photographs or illustrations.

✐ Consider many paths to becoming a book author. Carefully review collaborative projects or print-on-demand publishers. Research self-publishing to see whether it's a viable option rather than true subsidy presses.

✐ Be a proactive marketer, seeking (no creating!) any and all promotional opportunities for your book. Keep your name—or more important, the book's title—in the spotlight. Publishers desire authors who are vested and involved in the project's success.

Afterword

So, what do you think? After reading these chapters, do you have more possibilities to ponder for making money as a writer? I'm guessing that you do, and I wish you only the best in all your writing endeavors. May this book lead you down a very profitable writing path.

Some of the tasks here might seem easy and effortless while others might seem inappropriate or maybe even impossible given a lack of clips (or the right clips), education, or experience. But take it from my experience, if not your own—you never know where your writing career will lead you. Be prepared for new challenges and assignments to shape the days, months, and years ahead in ways you might never have imagined. Keep this book as a handy reference, for over the years, you may need the guidance, answers to new questions, or simply a spark of motivation.

Allow your skills to advance, not only with each assignment you garner, but with additional resources, networking, conferences, and classes. Often, you must spend money in order to make money, or advance to the next level. Soon you'll see the checks outnumbering the rejection notices, and your confidence will soar. Your occasional or part-time freelancing may suddenly become a full-time endeavor.

Thanks for reading and recommending this resource to others. I hope you're off to an inspiring and prosperous start! I'd love to hear your own innovative ways of making money as a writer. E-mail me at loriann@loriannoberlin.com.

Appendix: Writing Resources

Inspiration and Business Matters

Abbe, Elfrieda, ed., *The Writer's Handbook 2003,* Waukesha, Wis.: Kalmbach Publishing, 2002.

Bly, Robert W., *101 Ways to Make Every Second Count,* Franklin Lakes, N.J.: Career Press, 1999.

Brogan, Kathryn Struckel, and Robin Lee Brewer, eds., *Writer's Market,* Cincinnati, Ohio: Writer's Digest, 2003.

Conrad, Barnaby, and Monte Schulz, *Snoopy's Guide to the Writing Life,* Cincinnati, Ohio: Writer's Digest, 2002.

Devel, Jacqueline, *Publicize Your Book!* New York: Perigee, 2003.

Eberts, Marjorie, and Margaret Gisler, *Careers for Book Worms & Other Literary Types,* New York: McGraw-Hill, 2003.

Feiertag, Joe, Mary Carmen Cupito, and the editors of *Writer's Market, The Writer's Market Companion,* Cincinnati, Ohio: Writer's Digest, 2000.

Henderson, Kathy, *The Young Writer's Guide to Getting Published,* Cincinnati, Ohio: Writer's Digest, 2001.

Ideas for Great Home Offices, Menlo Park, Calif.: Sunset, 1995.

King, Stephen, *On Writing: A Memoir of the Craft,* New York: Scribner, 2000.

Kopelman, Alexander, *National Writer's Union Guide to Freelance Rates and Standard Practice,* Cincinnati, Ohio: Writer's Digest, 1995.

Kremer, John, *Celebrate Today,* Fairfield, Iowa: Open Horizons Publishing, 1995.

————, *1001 Ways to Market Your Books,* Fairfield, Iowa: Open Horizons Publishing, 2000.

Lerner, Betsy, *The Forest for the Trees: An Editor's Advice to Writers,* Riverhead, 2000.

Levinson, Jay Conrad, Rick Frishman, and Michael Larsen, *Guerrilla Marketing for Writers,* Cincinnati, Ohio: Writer's Digest, 2000.

Mogel, Leonard, *Careers in Communications and Entertainment,* New York: Kaplan Books, 2000.

Oberlin, Loriann Hoff, *Working at Home While the Kids Are There, Too,* Franklin Lakes, N.J.: Career Press, 1997.

Porter-Roth, Bud, *How to Respond & Win the Bid,* Grants Pass, Ore.: The Oasis Press, 1993.

Reeves, Jody, *Writing Alone, Writing Together: A Guide for Writers and Writing Groups,* Novato, Calif.: New World Library, 2002.

Rekulak, Jason, *The Writer's Block: 786 Ideas to Jump-Start Your Imagination*, Philadelphia, Pa.: Running Press, 2001.

Riha, John, ed., *Better Homes and Gardens Home Offices,* Des Moines, Iowa: Meredith, 1997.

Waller, James, *Freelance Writers' Guide,* New York: National Writers Union, 2000, distributed by Writer's Digest, Cincinnati, Ohio.

Writing and Style References

Amoss, Berthe, and Eric Suben, *The Children's Writer's Reference,* Cincinnati, Ohio: Writer's Digest, 1999.

Bass, Frank, *The Associated Press Guide to Internet Research & Reporting,* New York: Perseus, 2002.

Blake, Gary, and Robert W. Bly, *The Elements of Technical Writing,* New York: Macmillan, 1993.

Cappon, Rene J., *The Associated Press Guide to Newswriting,* Lawrenceville, N.J.: Arco, 2000.

The Chicago Manual of Style, 14th ed., Chicago, Ill.: University of Chicago Press, 1993.

English Grammar, English Punctuation and Writing Basics Video/DVD, Falls Church, Va.: Cerebellum Corporation, Standard Deviants Series, 2002.

Goldstein, Norm, *The Associated Press Stylebook and Briefing on Media Law,* New York: Perseus, 2002.

Hacker, Diana, *A Writer's Reference,* New York: Bedford/St. Martins Press, 2002.

Leland, Christopher T., *The Creative Writer's Style Guide*, Cincinnati, Ohio: Story Press, 2002.

Merriam-Webster's Collegiate Dictionary.

Mogilner, Alihandra, *Children's Writer's Word Book*, Cincinnati, Ohio: Writer's Digest, 1992.

Publication Manual of the American Psychological Association, Washington, D.C., APA, 2001.

Strunk Jr., William, *The Elements of Style*, New York: Macmillan, 2000.

Thurman, Susan, *The Everything Grammar and Style Book*, Avon, Mass.: Adams, 2002.

Webster's New World College Dictionary.

Webster's New World Roget's A–Z Thesaurus.

How-To/Fillers, Humor, Article, and Greeting Card References

Allen, Gary, *Resource Guide for Food Writers*, London & New York: Routledge, 1999.

Amende, Coral, *The Crossword Obsession*, New York: Berkley, 2001.

Burgett, Gordon, *Sell & Resell Your Magazine Articles*, Cincinnati, Ohio: Writer's Digest, 1997.

————, *Travel Writer's Guide*, Santa Maria, Calif.: Communication Unlimited, 2002.

Clark, Thomas, *Queries & Submissions*, Cincinnati, Ohio: Writer's Digest, 1995.

Cook, Marshall J., *Leads & Conclusions*, Cincinnati, Ohio: Writer's Digest, 1995.

DeSena, Carmine, *The Comedy Market: A Writer's Guide to Making Money Being Funny*, New York: Berkley, 1996.

Havelin, Michael, *Photography for Writers*, New York: Allworth Press, 1998.

Helitzer, Melvin, *Comedy Writing Secrets*, Cincinnati, Ohio: Writer's Digest, 1992.

Louden, Sandra M., *Write Well & Sell: Greeting Cards*, Pittsburgh, Pa.: Jam Packed Press, 1998.

Moore, Karen Ann, *You Can Write Greeting Cards*, Cincinnati, Ohio: Writer's Digest, 1999.

Ostman, Barbara Gibbs, and Jane Baker, *The Recipe Writer's Handbook*, Hoboken, N.J.: Wiley, 2001.

Perret, Gene, and Carol Burnett, *Comedy Writing Step by Step,* New York: Samuel French, 1990.

Poehner, Donna, *Photographer's Market,* Cincinnati, Ohio: Writer's Digest, 2004.

Vorhaus, John, *The Comic Toolbox,* Los Angeles, Calif.: Silman-James Press, 1994.

Wigand, Molly, *How to Write & Sell Greeting Cards, Bumper Stickers, T-Shirts and Other Fun Stuff,* Cincinnati, Ohio: Writer's Digest, 1992.

How-To/Teaching, Business, Technical, and Newsletter References

Beach, Mark, *Editing Your Newsletter,* Cincinnati, Ohio: Writer's Digest, 1995.

Bly, Robert W., *The Online Copywriter's Handbook,* New York: McGraw-Hill, 2002.

Curtis, Richard, and William Thomas Quick, *How to Get Your E-Book Published,* Cincinnati, Ohio: Writer's Digest, 2002.

Fanson, Barbara, *Start & Run a Profitable Desktop Publishing Business,* North Vancouver, British Columbia, Canada: Self-Counsel Press, 1997.

Floyd, Elaine, *Creating Family Newsletters,* Newsletter Resources, 1998.

————, *Marketing with Newsletters,* Cincinnati, Ohio: Writer's Digest, 2002.

Freed, Richard, Shervin Freed, and Joe Romano, *Writing Winning Business Proposals,* New York: McGraw-Hill, 2003.

Hamper, Robert L., and L. Sue Baugh, *Handbook for Writing Proposals,* New York: McGraw-Hill, 1995.

Herman, Jeff, *Writer's Guide to Book Editors, Publishers & Literary Agents,* Roseville, Calif.: Prima, 2003.

Herman, Jeff, and Deborah Levine Herman, *Write the Perfect Book Proposal: 10 That Sold and Why,* Hoboken, N.J.: Wiley, 2001.

Holtz, Herman, *Proven Proposal Strategies to Winning More Business,* Denver, Colo.: Upstart Publishing, 1998.

Holtz, Shel, *Public Relations on the Net,* New York: AMACOM Books, 2002.

Karasik, Paul, *How to Make It Big in the Seminar Business,* New York: McGraw-Hill, 1992.

Levine, Michael, *Guerrilla PR Wired*, New York: McGraw-Hill, 2002.

Levinson, Jay Conrad, Rick Frishman, and Jill Lublin, *Guerrilla Publicity*, Avon, Mass.: Adams, 2002.

Lewis, Jeff, and Dick Jones, *How to Get Noticed by the National Media*, Duluth, Minn.: Trellis Publishing, 2001.

Merriam, Sharan B., and Ralph G. Brockett, *The Profession & Practice of Adult Education*, New York: Jossey-Bass, 1997.

Parker, Roger C., *Desktop Publishing & Design for Dummies*, New York: Hungry Minds, 1995.

Podesta, Sandra, and Andrea Paxton, *201 Killer Cover Letters*, New York: McGraw-Hill, 2003.

Pope, Alice, ed., *Children's Writer's & Illustrator's Market*, Cincinnati, Ohio: Writer's Digest, 2002.

Ross, Tom and Marilyn, *The Complete Guide to Self-Publishing*, Cincinnati, Ohio: Writer's Digest, 2002.

Salisbury, Linda and Jim, *Smart Self-Publishing*, Charlotte Harbor, Fla.: Tabby House, 1997.

Shapiro, Ellen R., *Writer's and Illustrator's Guide to Children's Book Publishers and Agents*, Roseville, Calif.: Prima, 2002.

Sinclair, Joseph T., Lani W. Sinclair, PhD, and Joseph G. Lansing, *Creating Web-Based Training*, AMACOM, 2002.

Slaunwhite, Steve, *Start and Run a Copywriting Business*, Self-Counsel Press, 2001.

Tamblyn, Doni, *Laugh and Learn*, AMACOM Books, 2003.

Tedesco, Anthony and Paul, *Online Markets for Writers: How to Make Money by Selling Your Writing on the Internet*, New York: Owl Books, 2000.

Vater, Rachel, ed., *2003 Guide to Literary Agents*, Cincinnati, Ohio: Writer's Digest, 2003.

Walters, Dottie and Lilly, *Speak and Grow Rich*, Upper Saddle River, N.J.: Prentice Hall, 1997.

Whitcomb, Susan Britton, *Resume Magic: Trade Secrets of a Professional Resume Writer*, Indianapolis, Ind.: Jist Works, 2003.

Wilson, Arthur L., and Elisabeth R. Hayes, *Handbook of Adult & Continuing Education*, New York: Jossey-Bass, 2000.

Woodard, Cheryl, *Starting & Running a Successful Newsletter or Magazine*, Berkeley, Calif.: Nolo, 1996.

Yate, Martin John, *Resumes That Knock Em Dead*, Avon, Mass.: Adams, 2000.

Periodicals

Advertising Age
Editor & Publisher
Newswire
Public Relations Journal
Publisher's Weekly
Radio & Records
Standup and *Comedian's Registry*
The Writer
Writer's Digest

Web Sites and Organizations

http://fdncenter.org (The Foundation Center for nonprofit proposals/ grants)
www.amanet.org (American Management Association)
www.amwa.org (American Medical Writers Association)
www.asindexing.org (American Society of Indexers)
www.asja.org (American Society of Journalists and Authors)
www.asme.magazine.org (American Society of Magazine Editors)
www.authorsguild.org (Authors Guild)
www.bisg.org (Book Industry Study Group)
www.bookwire.com (book industry information)
www.comedyusa.com (for comedy industry guide)
www.crosswordweaver.com (Crossword Weaver software)
www.elibrary.com (Electronic Library Service)
www.freelancing4money.com (Freelancing 4 Money Web site/e-newsletter)
www.giftassoc.org (Gift Association of America)
www.giftwarenews.net (Giftware News)
www.google.com (arguably one of the best search engines)
www.grammarlady.com (answers your grammar questions)
www.grammarqueen.com (for grammar concerns)
www.greetingcard.org (Greeting Card Association)
www.greetingcardwriting.com (Sandra Louden/greeting cards)
www.iabc.com (International Association of Business Communicators)
www.libraryjournal.com and www.schoollibraryjournal.com (*Library Journal*)
www.nasw.org (National Association of Science Writers)
www.nwu.org (National Writers Union)

www.partylinepublishing.com (Party Line newsletter)
www.profnet.com (journalist research assistance)
www.prsa.org (Public Relations Society of America)
www.publisherslunch.com (book trade e-newsletter)
www.publishersweekly.com (*Publisher's Weekly*)
www.satw.org (Society of American Travel Writers)
www.stc.org (Society for Technical Communication)
www.the-efa.org (Editorial Freelancers Association)
www.toastmasters.org (Toastmasters public-speaking groups)
www.wordsearchmaker.com (1-2-3 Word Search Maker software)
www.writermag.com (*The Writer* magazine)
www.writersdigest.com (*Writer's Digest* magazine)
www.writerswrite.com/greetingcards (greeting card information)

Productivity

www.adobe.com
www.avery.com
www.broderbund.com
www.cerebellum.com
www.macromedia.com
www.mcafee.com
www.microsoft.com
www.quicken.com
www.roxio.com
www.symantec.com
www.turbotax.com
www.varietygames.com

Index

About the Author

Loriann Hoff Oberlin is a professional writer contributing to major magazines, regional publications, metropolitan newspapers, and newsletters across the country. She is the author of *Writing for Money, The Everything American History Book, The Insiders' Guide to Pittsburgh,* and *Surviving Separation and Divorce,* a book that is now published in Spanish. She served as the divorce pro on www.oxygen.com.

In collaboration with Dr. Tim Murphy, a member of the U.S. House of Representatives, she co-wrote *The Angry Child,* a timely book about childhood issues ranging from anxiety and depression to ordinary parenting problems and discipline.

Ms. Oberlin also wrote *Working at Home While the Kids Are There, Too.* Her monthly column on balancing work and family appeared in the *Pittsburgh Business Times.* She's also contributed to *Family Circle, Woman's Day, Pittsburgh Post-Gazette, Elegant Bride, Bridal Guide, Attaché, Parents, Woman's World, Working at Home, Good Times, Hemispheres,* and the *Saturday Evening Post,* among other publications.

Promoting her own work, she has appeared on radio talk shows and television newscasts, including the *CNN Morning News* and *Sally Jesse Raphael,* as well as at bookstores and conferences. Ms. Oberlin has taught writing workshops at writer's conferences, colleges, and universities in various states. She continues to teach these at the University of Pittsburgh, around Washington, D.C., and online via a distance-writing seminar she created with one-on-one feedback, using this book and other references. In addition to writing and teaching, she frequently speaks before groups of writers at conferences and book stores as well as before young writers in schools.

Ms. Oberlin resides in suburban Maryland, outside Washington, D.C., with her husband and two sons. To share your own money-making experiences, learn more about her online writing seminar, or merely comment upon this book, reach her in care of AMACOM Books, through her Web site at www.loriannoberlin.com, or by e-mailing her at loriann@loriannoberlin.com.